UNFINISHED BUSINESS

ROBIN JOHNSON

UNFINISHED BUSINESS

ESSAYS ON THE PSYCHOLOGICALLY INFORMED ENVIRONMENT

Fertile Imagination Press

Copyright © 2023 by Robin Johnson

All rights reserved. No part of this book may be reproduced in any manner whatsoever without written permission except in the case of brief quotations embodied in critical articles and reviews.

First Printing, 2023

CONTENTS

1 — Foreword
1

2 — Introduction
7

3 — Three models of the causes of homelessness, and their implications for the 'psychology' in services
21

4 — Trauma is not the only psychology: Adverse Childhood Experiences and the development of responsive services
46

5 — The Window of Tolerance, the Drama Triangle and the Adjacent Possible
65

6 — Attachment, trauma and the social environment: a bio-psycho-social perspective on homelessness work
79

7 — Strengths, ambivalence and paradox : groups, role taking and peer-to-peer accountability in a community therapeutic environment
94

CONTENTS

8 — Living in 'Temporary Accommodation' - is there a role for TIC and PIEs?
108

9 — Pre-treatment and PIEs in the micro-social world
133

10 — Unfinished business
153

11 — Afterthoughts
156

About the author
159

CHAPTER 1

FOREWORD

In a book of essays and other such non-fiction writings, it is customary for any more personal comments and reflections from the author to be safely corralled into the Foreword. Here by tradition we have 'thanks to all those who helped'; and 'any mistakes are my own' and so on.

This collection of essays, however, is more personal throughout. I will be re-tracing here much of my recent and past working life and career; and to my mind, that thread of a personal development is relevant. I mean not to look back here, or claim that these long roots give my writings any more authority; I mean simply to illustrate how for us all the process of learning is continuous. This, I think, is the underlying message of the PIE approach. It's a journey.

In the 'Introduction' chapter to these essays I intend to relate some history, and the gradual, on-going evolution of my own thinking and writing, from the late 1960s to the early summer months of 2023. This is how ideas actually come, in the course of living, in conversations; and in loose ends that sometimes one day turn out to be tied in, to enrich some other subject with a new angle. Nothing is wasted, just by being set aside for another time.

So in fact we can begin here at the end, the last few months, because in the title of this collection, *'Unfinished business',* I mean to reflect both its origins and its conclusion; or rather, its lack of conclusion. And there is a point to be made here.

'Unfinalisable'

My friend and colleague Ray has introduced me to a word for work that never ends, not because you do not get round to finishing it, but because that is the nature of the work; or in my case, the thinking about and describing of what is largely the work of others. He says some things are 'unfinalisable'; and that seems a good word for this work.

This book was originally going to be a small selection of unpublished and often unfinished articles, half-written drafts on an eclectic range of subjects that I had been working on, or wanting to work on, at the point where, in the Spring of 2022, I had to pause in my work.

As that year began, I found that there was good reason to suspect that I was going to need some medical treatment. If so, although most likely treatable, the treatment itself was at least likely to be somewhat debilitating. Yet I was, after all, in my mid-70s; and had been saying for years that I must step back at some point. Surely I had reached my 'best before' date?

So on first hearing this news, I had thought it wise to start to tidy up my desk, preparing things as best I could to hand over my work to a next generation emerging, who could take forward some of what I had begun. We now have a good handful of colleagues keen to carry on some of the work of the PIElink website, (www.pielink.net) which has become the focus of much of my efforts. I believe they will do good things. My thanks to you all.

With luck, good care, good friends and colleagues, and good morale, I am able to pass on much of this work now, to step back and to hand over the reins. Nevertheless I have always said that I don't expect to 'retire' as such, but rather to move on to other things; and a proper illness has just given me the hint, the natural marker of the moment to do so.

My role model here has been the Cheshire Cat from Alice in Wonderland. The cat, you will recall, sits perched high in a tree; and being a talking cat - of course - it converses with Alice, commenting somewhat mischievously on the action below. After a while, the cat gradually fades away - leaving the grin behind. A little while later, the cat re-materializes for a few more comments, before fading again; but always *leaving the grin behind.*

That was my plan.

Timing

As Spring turned to Summer, I found there was a long delay in getting a final diagnosis. I had yet to go through a series of tests and procedures, like some perverse game of 'It's a Knock Out', in which the contestants hope at each stage to be taken out, and not have to go on to the next stage. Over this time I set about adjusting all the material on the PIElink, which would then be a legacy to look back on.

As Summer then turned to Autumn, and I waited for a date for the active treatment stage to begin, I found I had time on my hands; and as I worked on tidying the website's pages I began to think it could also make sense to try to write up and publish in book from some thoughts on the general direction of my work, a kind of 'swan song' - maybe something like a beginners' guide to PIEs. Over several months that too began to take shape.

However I also had these half a dozen or more articles, think pieces, notes for future presentations that I had never managed to finish to my own satisfaction. These were not sufficiently polished for publication in a journal, for example, after which I could add them to the PIElink library.

The long and iterative process of peer review, not to mention the painstaking work of detailing all references in a required format, is protracted and time-consuming. Although it may be necessary for publication in any academic journal, to then add to the 'literature' on PIEs, it is not particularly satisfying in itself. I didn't have the heart for it.

So these pieces, I thought, were likely to remain as... unfinished business. If I was serious about taking this as the moment to retire, I did not expect to have the time or the inclination to finish them.

Yet over this period I was in correspondence still with a few colleagues, asking my thoughts on one thing or another on subjects on which, as it happens, I already had these writings in draft and good enough to share, however unpolished. I would send them a draft, explaining that it was unfinished; and I began to think it was a bit of a shame and a waste to share these unfinished pieces with just a few friends.

And then, as it so happens, it turned out that there be a long preparatory stage before starting treatment; and this gave me first weeks, then months, that I did not expect. Now I had both reason and time to look again at these bits and pieces; against expectations, I found I had the energy and the motivation to continue working on a few, trying to get them to say what I really wanted to say. The collection even grew.

But then I had a thought: why does everything have to be polished? In a somewhat impish 'demob' mood I decided that, with limited time, I could simply publish these essays unfinished, if I wrote them as chapters in a book that I might self-publish, where the demands of academic or commercial publishers are not enforced. The idea of publishing these as a collection of 'unfinished' pieces, with this as the title, came initially from that.

This is that book.

Writing in real time

But then the stage of active treatment was surprisingly kind, in giving me relatively few side effects to deal with. I began to feel a little sheepish over having perhaps over-reacted. There was, it seemed, 'life in the old dog yet'.

Meanwhile, in the course of writing the book on PIEs, and thinking to also make it an introduction to the PIElink, I had conceived the idea of having pages on the website matching chapters in the book. Rather than having constant references in the book, clogging up the pages, or a references page at the end, I could have links to the pages of the website. Here readers could come across new material, including links to video, or to forums where the discussions could continue.

The 'introduction' book is now finished, and it is called *'Psychologically informed environments from the ground up: Service design for complex needs'*; and is now published. But the idea of linking chapters in a book to pages on the site seems just as neat for this book as for that. Then all this work could continue to grow, to be 'unfinalised'.

* * *

That said, I do hope the various pieces in this collection each stand as writings in their own right; and as a collection I think they do hang together, as I will try to bring out in the 'Introduction' chapter. At least in their own way they tell a story of the breadth of issues that I have tried to touch upon and to bring together into the project that became, in effect, my life's work: the development and promotion of PIEs.

'Unfinished business', though, still seems to me a good phrase to describe what I see as my contribution up to this point to a project that I had myself launched and steered thus far; but which should continue to evolve after my stepping back. As I will say in the Introduction, I would not want my thoughts at this stage to be taken as the last word on the subject; that would in fact be the opposite of what I intended.

The grin remains.

Robin Johnson,

September 2023,
Falmouth, Cornwall

CHAPTER 2

INTRODUCTION

Range, threads, and convergence

This collection of essays represents some fresh thoughts on a wide range of issues and perspectives related to the work of developing psychologically informed environments. Some of them could do with more work; but perhaps they always would. At least linking these chapters with pages on the PIElink website, as I describe in the Foreword, allows these thoughts to continue to unfold. There is no 'last word' on these subjects.

There is a narrative of sorts here; but there are also separate stands, interweaving. Some I will point out; some I will leave it to the reader to discover. Nevertheless, underneath the breadth and diversity in these roaming thoughts, I do think there is a degree of coherence, even a convergence; and I will try to use this 'Introduction' chapter to tease this out.

In general, most essays here focus on the 'psychology' - broadly defined - involved in practice. Some dig a little deeper into the roots of the thinking, whether in the early history of social psychiatry, or in the development of a more scientific understanding of humans and their environments.

A couple of them do include an introduction to the PIEs 2.0 framework, which may be helpful for those that may come new to this approach. But in each case they approach the application of the framework from different and somewhat new angles. In this way they should hopefully complement rather than duplicate the accounts that readers will find in the other essays, or on the PIElink, the community of practice website (www.pielink.net).

Hopefully this will not seem too repetitive for those already familiar with this, but instead may help to shed new light on the flexibility of this framework. For those not so familiar, I would definitely suggest reading around the website - bearing in mind that there is also another book which is published at the same time as this one, intended as more of a general introduction to PIEs.

The title of that book is: *Psychologically Informed Environments from the ground up: Service design for complex needs*', and just as you will find pages on the PIElink that match the chapters of this book, and so allow the discussion here to be 'unfinalised', the same is true of the other. You will find matching pages to the chapters in that book, too, on the website; and from there, links to all manner of specific issues that may interest any reader on PIEs. You will find the links to both books in the PIElink pages on 'PIE publications'.

* * *

Three models of the origins of homelessness, and their implications for the 'psychology' in services

The first of these essays began life as a conversation with a stranger in a pub, which I later turned into a video, with a wry humour on a serious subject - my trademark, I'd like to think. Because the subject IS serious, and the analysis seems worth sharing, I had thought of converting it into a publishable account for an academic or research journal, as a contribution to the literature that search engines would then come across. But I simply ran out of time.

I am surely best known in homelessness circles for arguing that homelessness services need a quite acute awareness of the 'psychological' needs of their service users, which many of them, I argue, in fact do show. But I am studiously neutral as to what 'psychology' is appropriate to use and besides, for my own part I am always interested in seeing things from another angle.

In this essay, conscious of the charge that we may at times be 'psychologising' and 'pathologising' where that is not necessarily helpful, I wanted to explore the implications and the potential strengths in *not* seeing homelessness as necessarily a manifestation of past trauma, to see what else this can show. In suggesting three models, I am perhaps overstating the difference between them. But I hope that helps to make the point.

Adding in two alternative views, like a varifocal lens, allows us to see more clearly the psychological and emotional issues (sic) that arise in an area such as 'Living in Temporary Accommodation' - 'TA' - that had not really received a lot of attention until now in discussions of the psychology in services.

Yet here we have a growing number of individuals, in the UK and elsewhere, for whom the state has been obliged to provide a supposedly 'temporary' solution. In 'the good times' TA can indeed be simply temporary and transient. But when times are harder, as the economic model describes, it is then all too easy for this timeless zone called 'temporary' to extend apparently without limit.

Then there is the risk of becoming stranded, and 'lost in space', as a result of 'Swiss cheese' model holes in the system, and it becomes ever harder to find a way out. There are then psychological and emotional issues here that are a mixture of those from the economics and the Swiss Cheese models. The complexity in these 'complex needs' lies not in the individual, however, but in the system that has parked them there.

Trauma is not the only psychology: Adverse Childhood Experiences and the development of more responsive services

The second essay takes up and continues the point at which 'three models' ends: my claim there is that the most successful of homelessness services not only need to be, but actually are, quite versatile and responsive. They have to be willing and able to flex to the needs, ambitions and strengths of each new individual, with whatever understandings they can muster - 'eclectic' is the more theoretical term, if you wish. In this essay, I'll be looking at how they can, and do.

The essay begins with one of the most widespread and currently most keenly adopted theories of vulnerability - Adverse Childhood Experiences (or ACEs) and what is often seen as its practical expression in practice, Trauma Informed Care -

and starts with the genuine usefulness of this analysis, drawn largely from public health accounts. These echo the case that we had made for their being high levels of 'complex trauma' in the homelessness population in the UK government's guidance documents on homelessness from 2010 and 2012, on which I was one of the co-authors.

That document in 2010 was the first government-endorsed guidance to use this new phrase, 'a psychologically informed environment'. As I go on to tease out in this essay, the public health analysis is very readily compatible with the PIEs framework that then eventually evolved from that first guidance. What is different in the analysis here is that it questions the faith that many people currently place in neuroscience, as the explanation of the behavioural consequences of ACEs.

Some of the earliest research to make these links was, with hindsight, quite alarmist in tone, suggesting that the wiring of the traumatised brain would then be permanently set in dysfunctional patterns. The implication - quite often asserted as a scientific fact - was that without early intervention to intercept and remedy the trauma, it would then be too late to change people's behaviour.

One of my concerns is that the neuroscience sometimes has a tendency to be quite reductionist in its view of human beings and one dimensional in its view of human potential. I am also conscious that this trauma narrative usually allows little scope for the phenomenon of post-traumatic growth; or for exploration of how to assist in that growth. Yet this is just what we do see, in work with adults. That scope is precisely what we work with.

A growing concern I have - not covered in the original essay, so I must add it now - arises when we find trauma presented not just as one useful source of insights, but as *the* expected framework for an understanding of all service users' issues. Psychologists are conscious of the impact of 'priming' a discussion with ideas that then colour the discussion that follows, leading the witness. To foreground issues of past trauma - let alone to presuppose them - can lead us to focus on these issues, that we think must matter. But this is not necessarily what the individual in front of us wants - or wants from us.

Another concern, linked to that, is that the trauma narrative tends to paint with the same brush all 'service users' in homelessness. As we'll see for example later, in the essay on living in temporary accommodation, this is simply not the case. But the trauma narrative can also lead to a simplistic account in which people are then too readily cast, especially by a sensationalist media and some un-wary educators, as victims: and this is the issue that the next article then takes on.

The Window of Tolerance, the Drama Triangle and the Adjacent Possible

This title of this essay may sound like the title of a Peter Greenaway film, and in fact this was originally to appear in the form of a video. This is a medium in which the use of infographics and colour for visualisations of complex issues would have been the natural thing to do. In this essay, I bring together three different insights that I find particularly useful, especially in combination.

One is from psychology (more accurately, from psychotherapy) and two from quite different areas of biology. The first is the well-known fight/flight response to threat, which does seem to be hard-wired into all creatures, and not just in us, the humans with our more sophisticated and pliable brains. In a couple of other essays, I will be exploring more of the biological roots of the human capacity for traumatising experience. The second is something yet more ancestral, which - or so it is claimed - applies not just to living creatures, but to all matter. Big picture thinking does not get much bigger.

Incidentally, for this account of the drama triangle I have also co-opted and 're-purposed' one of the sections from a chapter in a much earlier book, *'Complex Traumas and Its Effects: Perspectives on creating an environment for recovery'*, co-edited with Rex Haigh. (Full details via the 'PIE publications' pages on the PIElink; and now that I have created a page on the PIElink for selected extracts from this earlier book, you can find and read the whole chapter there.)

Attachment, stress and the social environment: a bio-psycho-social perspective on homelessness service's work

Meanwhile, if I may have suggested earlier some reservations about the excess of faith that we place in neuroscience as the most reliable underlying explanation of traumatised lives, the next essay now provides a counterbalance.

Here we pan back to look at the science behind environmental approaches, and in particular a different take on the neuroscience that underlies a lot of the current theories of trauma. Rather than cautioning over the simplistic over-use of neuroscience in trauma psychology - as I do in both the ACEs and the Window/Triangle papers earlier - here I take a far more positive view of what the science can really tell us.

Yet still the same conclusions emerge: that we must learn from experience - action learning - and not just from what we are told ought to work, just because whatever it may be is said to work somewhere else. Above all else, it's all about the relationships, not the models.

If caution and ambivalence over the role of explicitly therapeutic intent is beginning to emerge as a connecting thread between many of these articles, the next in this collection explores precisely that issue.

Strengths, ambivalence and paradox: groups, role taking and peer-to-peer accountability in a community therapeutic environment

Now we start by looking back fully 50 years, to my first experiences of working in mental health at the Henderson Hospital. Then as now, this has been seen as the archetypal therapeutic community, or 'TC'; and I am interested in what we might learn from applying this thinking about TCs, with hindsight, to a much wider range of environments and group processes.

This essay, too, began life as a conversation. In this case, it was a Zoom call with some people in the United States who wanted to create a specialist village community for people recovering from homelessness and addiction. These good folk proposed using the 'democratic therapeutic community' ('DTC') model.

As its name perhaps suggests, in a democratic TC it is 'horizontal' or 'peer-to-peer' accountability that is the cornerstone of the community (plus, typically, some appropriate form of psychotherapy). This is what distinguishes this model from the more hierarchical model of accountability that tended to apply in the communities known as 'concept TCs' - those which developed out of substance abuse self-help communities around the same time in the US.

All this had been my own starting point as a practitioner theorist, some 50 years earlier; and I had in fact written about this before; it was the subject of my Master's degree dissertation, which is still available to read, in the PIElink library. I think it was my ability to spot and articulate what I saw as this therapeutic and community thinking, and how its underlying themes were emerging spontaneously in social housing and homelessness services, that launched my later career as a social policy theorist and writer on PIEs.

I was invited to join this call to make the connection between what we had learned in the development of 'TCs' and what had been developing in homelessness services in the UK. But hearing what these US colleagues were planning reminded me of an aspect of life at the Henderson Hospital in the 1970s that is not often described, let alone analysed. It was really only when I began to write about it that the much wider relevance for services became evident.

Incidentally, you will see that, like the trauma/ACEs paper, this essay has the outline of a 'structured abstract'. This is because I was thinking to publish this perhaps in a therapeutic community journal, wanting to get into print. However, as the point of writing is that these issues go far beyond the small circles of social psychiatry journal readers, it actually seems better to include this article instead in a book with a far wider range. The resulting title will hopefully convey enough to whet the appetites of a few.

Note also that I have called these efforts not 'therapeutic communities' - that term being already taken - but instead have coined a new term, 'community therapeutic environments', for those services that may or may not see themselves as explicitly 'therapeutic', but are nevertheless developing ways of working that may make good use of the same social dynamics. I'd like to think that perhaps we might one day see 'community therapeutic environments' as the bridge between 'therapeutic communities' and PIEs.

* * *

The next three chapters return us to the present day, first to explore the ways that the PIEs approach aims to encompass and integrate a range of other ways of working within one overall framework; and then where we might be going next.

Living in 'Temporary Accommodation': is there a role for TIC and PIEs?

The next essay considers an entirely new area for the PIEs idea and framework: the situation of families 'placed' in temporary accommodation, and the work of the TAAGs, the locality-based 'temporary accommodation action groups', formed to lobby for better responses to a population whose needs do not fit the mould of other homelessness services' core clientele.

This essay was first written taking the form of a briefing for staff, produced for the Transitional Accommodation Action Network (TAAN). But since this full extended version is no longer brief, it may hopefully be useful to include it here as an example of the use of the thinking and the framework; and the TAAN team will take brier excerpts from it for their own use.

Nevertheless it takes the questioning, exploratory attitude which will continue, I hope, to be the hallmark of the PIE approach, as 'a way of seeing'. I see this exercise therefore not as an assessment or a measure of the effectiveness or suitability of TAAGs as PIEs, let alone of temporary accommodation. Instead it seems to me a test of the wider applicability of the PIEs framework itself.

The revised and expanded PIEs formulation, PIEs 2.0, was explicitly designed to be more comprehensive than the earlier 'classic' model had been, in order to reach into areas that the original version did not touch on. This was to include, for example, Trauma-Informed Care, and Housing First, which both by then were already becoming influential as new approaches to homelessness and complex needs. PIEs 2.0 attempted to include them as approaches.

But how far is this PIEs model really able to shed light on an aspect of homelessness that was not within its original scope, nor for that matter in TIC and HF? How far can either of these really help us to identify and to work on areas that are relevant to these networks and these services' kind of work?

I have suggested, earlier in this Introduction, that here we will need a mixture of the 'psychologies' of the economics and the Swiss Cheese models. In this chapter I try to take that suggestion a little further, into the practical application of these understandings.

Pre-treatment and PIEs in the micro-social world

Throughout this collection several strands interweave. There is the narrative of the development of the ideas in the PIE as 'a way of seeing'; there is the attempt to explore the practical application of the PIEs framework in a variety of contexts; and there are some issues of a more theoretical or scientific interest. This last essay has all three.

It continues the story of the evolution of the PIEs framework, past and future, and then also weaves in some quite new ideas on the nature of the subjective environment, continuing the more theoretical and scientific analysis of the bio-psycho-social world, before looking to the future, to where both PIEs and pretreatment are now reaching wider.

It begins with my first encounter with pretreatment. Coming across Jay Levy's work was one of the turning points in the development of the wider, more inclusive framework of ideas and practice that became PIEs 2.0. I have written about this already in several pages on the PIElink, and also in the chapters that I had contributed to the book that we co-edited, *'Cross-cultural Dialogues on Homelessness: From Pretreatment Strategies to Psychologically Informed Environments'*. Here I had talked of finding 'the common skills of engagement', as the common ground between one-to-one work and our development of holistic, 'in the round' approaches in PIEs.

The pretreatment approach is steadily gaining adherents now in the UK; but I feel there is more that we can do, to tease out the common essence in the PIEs and in this approach to individual engagement; something more that best expresses the intention and the need to recognise the lifeworld of the other - in this case, the chronically excluded person that we wish to engage, in homelessness outreach work.

Here I have attempted to do so by introducing what is to me a new concept, the 'Umwelt', that suggests that we can also see 'the environment' from an experiential angle - and this may then be the common thread. This is an exciting new idea, a quite new perspective on human capacities, and one which again roots human experience in the biological nature of our species, but from a new angle entirely.

Had I known of this concept earlier, I might have tried to work in a reference in the chapter on the bio-psycho-social perspective, where it belongs. But I had only just come across this concept when I wrote this pretreatment essay, originally as a chapter for Jay's next book.

Here it seemed relevant enough to make mention, however briefly and tantalisingly. But there is plenty more to explore here, and some of this exploration will continue on the PIElink, from the pages that refer to this book.

Unfinished business

This collection ends with a non-ending. Following the principle of of 'unfinalisability', this final chapter is not an essay itself, but a last comment, a confirmation that the PIElink site now has a page where we can continue the discussion and develop new material, new ideas, new directions.

Then, as if to bring home this point more fully, in the middle of August, just as I am tidying up these texts for publication, my colleague Natalie sends me a link to an article that appears in this months' issue of The Psychologist magazine. This article introduces a new concept, auto-ethnography, with a searing critique of the way that psychology research is conducted, published and taught.

I can't even begin here to write about how beautifully this heartfelt challenge to methodological orthodoxy chimes with so many of the themes I have been trying to tease out in much of my recent writing. I must leave it to the reader, and the future, to open this out.

So this last chapter is best seen not as a conclusion, but as a portal to another world - in this case, to the PIElink website, where these explorations and discussions can continue; and be fully unfinalisable...

CHAPTER 3

THREE MODELS OF THE CAUSES OF HOMELESSNESS, AND THEIR IMPLICATIONS FOR THE 'PSYCHOLOGY' IN SERVICES

With this essay, the first in this collection, I am going to outline what I take to be the three principal current models (or theories, or accounts) of the origins and nature of homelessness. I will then attempt to tease out from these models the implications for homelessness services, in terms of how they may best respond to the psychological and emotional issues that arise for their potential 'service users', as seen through the lens of each model.

By homelessness, and by 'service users', I mean all those who find themselves homeless, and so may come to the attention of homelessness services, whatever the kind or stage of homelessness in each case. This will include those we describe as 'hidden homeless' - those who have no home of their own, and are dependent on others for accommodation, in so far as the homelessness services are broadly aware of them as a group, if not as individuals.

I make no further attempt to define homelessness; and I do appreciate that this may mean ignoring for the moment - or at least, taking as read - some quite valuable work that has been done in recent years to identify in greater detail the many kinds and profiles of this highly heterogenous population of individuals. But we will be returning to this important issue of differentiation later in this analysis.

In real world situations, outside the conference hall or the academic paper, we do need to be able to give an account of the work that we do to the ordinary people whom we might encounter. Whether in a café, on a bus, or indeed on a park bench, if we are to communicate with others outside our specialist field, we need to be able to make the key points with broad-brush generalisations, and with whatever is to hand – in this case, quite literally.

The original version of this essay in fact arose from a conversation with a stranger in a pub; and to describe what we are all working on, I had used a paper napkin, my fingers and a piece of cutlery to illustrate the complexity, with a couple of (completely) imaginary graphs. Later I reworked this as a video, which is still available to watch, on the PIElink website. Sadly, neither the dynamics of the narrative nor the wry humour in this will work on the printed page; though you may yet spot some vestiges here in the text, showing through.

Nor is the bravado of an over-simplifying account – or three – my natural mode of analysis. But the reason for attempting this in print nonetheless is partly that, for a more specialist readership, it is worth going into more depth than my imaginary graphs could manage, and here is the opportunity.

Each of these accounts of course is an over-simplification; and in fact each contains within it elements of the others. But another reason, as I hope to explore here, is that by over-simplifying the case for each account, it may help to clarify some of the differing perspectives and the sheer complexities of the work that many services are tackling. In the concluding discussion section I will be looking at how services need to be - and in fact typically are – geared up for a much richer picture, especially as it applies to each actual individual; and the challenges that then arise for staff, in trying to do so.

Finally, at a time when there is growing public concern over homelessness, we do find the public conversation – and sometimes some academic discourse – conducted on these somewhat over-stated lines; and it is important to be able to engage with these discussions with some clarity.

But before I go on, we need one further word of clarification. I myself am probably best known in the world of homelessness services for having introduced the term 'psychologically informed environment', or 'PIE'. But I have always insisted that 'the psychology' in services is not, or need not be, a specialist discipline in which certain people are more expert than others by virtue of some specialist training.

When I speak here of 'psychology', I am not referring to research or clinical psychology, helpful though that sometimes may be. Instead, by 'psychology' I mean our understanding of the emotions and thinking, the past experience, of the individuals we encounter; and our everyday attempts, as fellow humans, to understand each other with 'ordinary psychology', 'emotional intelligence', or active empathy.

What I am taking about, both in PIEs and here, is this natural psychology that we are all born with, the capacity for understanding that we all have and constantly use – unless its driven out of us – and the ordinarily extra-ordinary capacity for empathy that we all use, in our day-to-day dealings with those we meet.

So now, with just these relatively simple conceptual and presentation tools, I will endeavour to illustrate those three theories of the origins of homelessness that I want to outline.

***

The economics model

The first model is what we can call the economic, or economics, model. That is, in this account it is economic forces, and in particular stark economic inequality, which is the core issue to understand and to address. The greater the degree of social and economic inequality, the more we will see people falling into homelessness.

In any society we see degrees of wealth, from the super-rich at the very top to those merely millionaires, gradually descending through the quite secure and comfortable to the 'just about coping'; and further down still, the more precarious, those with no buffer zone of resources and who live from payday to payday; and finally, those without even that.

In this analysis, wealth is the essential protective factor; and financial insecurity the principal risk. When times are good, in an economy of plenty, there's work and opportunity for all, there's housing for all, and there's support for those who might otherwise be left behind. Those without wealth to fall back on, those in the rental sector, may be living in technically temporary contractual accommodation, but there is no reason to worry. In my (imaginary) graph, there is a horizontal line for extreme poverty and destitution; but in times of plenty, no-one need fall below the line.

As hard times are coming, this line rises like an in-coming tide. When the line rises higher still, you have an economy approaching freefall. The comfortable are feeling less secure, and in a failing economy the competition for scant resources is becoming fierce. The financially precarious are struggling to meet their bills, and some now find themselves 'insecurely housed'. Some are going under, if only temporarily - for them homelessness is episodic, or intermittent; but not necessarily recurrent. But for those with the least resources of all, however, these episodes of homelessness get harder to pull out from. We have a population who now who may become 'entrenched'

If this sorry state continues you may have a build-up of long-standing decay, damage, neglect of the infrastructure. Now there's no resources to do anything to support the weaker members. (Some of us have been seeing an economy like this for quite a while.) And now there are more and more people who then find themselves sinking, going under, and unable to rise out. We have a growing population who are now entrenched.

In this account, therefore, the risk or likelihood of homelessness is seen as essentially an issue of the state of the economy and the financial precariousness of individuals. That is not to say, of course, that those who propose the economics analysis are claiming that there is no significant role for mental health issues in the vulnerability of those most precarious, nor a need for concern, compassion and support. It's just that they are in short supply, and the quality of strain is not mercy.

But in this model, these psychological and personal issues are secondary to the power of economic forces. Individual and personal characteristics may compound the situation; but the real problem is the state of the economy; and the collateral damage that is done to individuals is really another further aspect of the damage and the decay of the infrastructure.

This is certainly one way of looking at the causes and the nature of homelessness; and certainly when we are looking at the huge growth of homelessness in the last few years in the UK, for example, you would have to say that the failure of the economy to thrive after years of austerity, and cuts in benefits and support services as a consequence, have had a major impact. Although many will argue - as we will see in the next model - that adverse childhood experiences (ACEs) may predispose some individuals to such ills as homelessness in later life, no-one I think would try to suggest that there was a sudden increase in ACEs approximately 20 years ago, to account for the numbers we now see living on our streets.

Even with some allowance for the mental health issues that are now bound up with homelessness, according to the economics theory it can happen to anyone - anyone can fall through the safety net. Anyone could end up at the bottom of that line, or below.

The vulnerability model

The second common way of looking at homelessness takes the converse view. That is to say yes, there is truth in that argument that economic factors are significant, and recent pressures and cuts in services have made matters infinitely worse. But we do need to look at the particular vulnerability of some; and services need to address that. Some people are particularly vulnerable and struggle to keep themselves above water; and with limited personal resources, they struggle then to get back out when they fall through; and this is due to quite personal characteristics that we cannot ignore.

Seen through the vulnerability lens, the work of addressing homelessness is primarily about the health of the individual, rather than the health of the economy.

Where in the economic account at the very top of the pyramid we had the affluent, in the vulnerability thesis here have the shiny happy people. These are the ones that Maslow's hierarchy of self-actualization was about. These ones are creative, buzzing, getting on with things in their life. They also have friends, people they can turn to, they have enriching and rewarding relationships with everybody it seems.

To borrow, for a moment, an economics metaphor, they have masses of social capital. Whereas down at the bottom on this notional scale we find the people with very poor mental health. This means not necessarily outright mental illness, but people who have huge problems in living, dysfunctional behaviour, self-defeating relationships; and they may have attitudes to match - it's not just the behaviour, it is also the way you think about the world. These people are often quite alienated and sometimes even quite alienating. We sometimes used to call them 'the hard to engage' - although in a more enlightened era we tend to turn the phrase around, and say that they 'pose a challenge to services', and see this as the problem of those services, rather than of the individuals.

But in this population you will certainly find a lot of distrust of services, a lot of despair, very poor self-image, difficulties in the family, perhaps. These may make that person more likely to fall through society's informal as well as the formal safety nets, with an erosion of precisely that social capital that is protective for so many people - even the more affluent.

So in hard times here we might have had a graph where - just as in the economics graph - we see more and more people at risk of falling through the cracks. It is certainly still true that economic forces will add to the pressures on all citizens; and the children of the affluent or the comfortable may also be feeling that pressure. But unless drugs or other self-medications start to complicate the picture, they are much less likely to fall quite so far, or stay down for quite so long.

* * *

Here then are two quite coherent but quite different versions of how people may end up homeless, whether temporarily or chronically mired in homelessness. A lot of the rhetoric surrounding these services tends to go in one or other of these different directions, sometimes both at the same time. But in practice the people at the bottom are pretty much the same, either way.

Nevertheless, there is a third account - and for this one we need a new way to illustrate the issue – not a graph here, but actually a metaphor which is fortunately a familiar image.

The Swiss Cheese model

The third commonly held model is the one I will call, for simplicity, the Swiss Cheese model. Although it is not often called this, this is an image that is fairly well know and fairly immediately intelligible. This model sees the likelihood of falling into homelessness, and becoming increasingly trapped, as not just a factor of the characteristics of individuals, or even of whole macro-economic forces, but a matter of risks, safety nets and system coherence – or lack of it.

The Swiss cheese model of accidents and risk was developed, I believe, originally in the air traffic industry, where they had to identify how accidents, however rare, do still happen. In air traffic accidents, and many other forms of accident, a whole string of fail-safes have to fail, all at the same unfortunate moment, for anyone to fall through them all. This model is now also used in other areas of security - like computer security - where people with malicious intent seek to probe weak spots and possible entry points in systems, and penetrate through a number of different defences, to find a chink in the armour.

This model or explanation focusses not so much on the characteristics of particular individuals, but the quality of the safety net. Statistical likelihood of precariousness or vulnerability is now no longer the key issue – it's the outliers that count - which is why a simple graph with either of the previous two 'quantifiable values' is no longer a useful visualisation.
 What is needed is an understanding not of general risk and likelihood, but of quite specific and unusual circumstances, and an unfortunate combination or sequence of specific circumstances.

We may have a whole string of different nets and safety nets, but the fail-safes fail to save in an individual instance. If there are some 'first line' safety nets in place and if they are robust enough, then rather than falling through, the individual meets one of these fail-safes and they bounce back. Like a fly caught in a window pane, it may be hard to see the way out at first; but if they do, they get back into the swirl of life, the ebbs and flows and so on.

They aren't particularly damaged or entrenched, nor are they plunged into whatever it is that is at the end of what they've fallen through –in this instance, since we are focussed on homelessness, we might be thinking of sofa-surfing; or a few nights on the streets, before finding a support service.

But the risk is that whilst bouncing around, trying to find the way back, they may fall through not just one safety net, but then another. It has been estimated that it takes as little as two weeks of sleeping on the streets to flip into rough sleeping as a habit, a lifestyle – which is a measure of how adaptable we humans are, and how willing to make the best of our situations. In a well ordered system, there may be yet another service that may catch them; but we are now entering the world of the more entrenched.

Becoming entrenched is therefore partly a question of how many nets there are and how robust they are, how wide the gaps to fall through, and how many. It's also partly a reflection of how steep the fall is, as people fall through the nets. It's only if they are all aligned together, these holes, that you risk falling through them all in one go; this is the Swiss cheese as applied in air traffic accidents, for example. But that is why it is still possible to do so.

For some people falling through the net can be very, very rapid indeed. But for others it's a much slower process of pinging to and fro perhaps, and getting stuck in some kind of intermediate demi-monde - not fully out, not fully in yet. Then the key issue is just as much about how well joined up the various different support services may actually be, or may need to be; and if the gaps cluster in a particular area, so that that's the area where people are most likely to fall through. It's now about how this is spotted by the people who plan and manage support services.

* * *

So, here we have our three principle theories - the economics theory, the vulnerability theory and the swiss cheese theory of risk and luck. What then is the significance of these three different understandings for the experience of ending up homeless and for the 'psychology' that homelessness services aiming for engagement must work with?

Psychology in the economics model

If you take on board the economics theory, what people primarily need is practical help. If suddenly homeless, they are going to need a roof overnight. This is the bottom rung of Maslow's hierarchy of needs, and they're going to need those fundamental needs met. They are then going to need some help and advice to get back in the swing of things: help with benefits, maybe (in some jurisdictions such as in the United States) some kind of specialist voucher system, for example, to assist people in getting back into the housing market.

Or they might need referral on, in some cases, to other specialist services that can provide help. But if they're needing referral on, it's because that's what every citizen has the right to. This is not even necessarily to do with being homeless - homelessness is just a temporary circumstance. But anybody has a right to other services. So if there's to be any 'psychology' involved in this at all, it's about the dignity of rights, and of citizenship. It's about having and keeping some kind of pride and self-respect.

In terms of psychological models, probably most relevant here is the strengths model - saying let's not look at what this person cannot do, let's not look at them in terms of their current (or assumed) deficits, but let's look at them in terms of their strengths and their potential for recovery. For any more formal theory, if at all, you will probably be drawing on broadly a humanistic psychology approach, which is about values, aspiration, what people find meaningful in their lives.

At all costs, what you would not do is add to an already bruised self-image, and compound the stigma with which people are already quite likely to be seeing themselves by talking about *their* particular vulnerability. We want to ensure that the person hasn't got stuck into a dysfunctional lifestyle that will then mean that failing to help them in their hour of need may cause other difficulties that will cost the state in other ways – health and crime in particular

Because mental health is seen as secondary, in this account the case for developing support services here is primarily an economic case. You want to get people back on their feet as soon as possible, after a blip on the screen. You can also make the economic case that there are some quite significant cost savings to the public purse from such damage limitation.

People here are essentially economic entities; and as such, as resources, they are being wasted. This may sound callous, but this is an argument that some theorists and funders have made, trying to convince other funders – usually government – that prevention is actually a good investment.

But effectively you're arguing that we want to get this person back into being a productive citizen and out of their run of bad luck as fast as possible, because it can happen to anyone. Anyone can fall through those nets.

Psychology in the vulnerability model

The alternative theory - what I have called the vulnerability approach - focusses instead on the levels of poor mental health of the individuals that we do tend to find in this population. Admittedly these are often mental health problems that on the whole mental health services do not see (and certainly treatment services often don't effectively engage with them - which is why they don't see them).

So these are the areas where homelessness services can - and do - develop skills and processes for engaging people that other services have been unable to do. We need to talk here, therefore, about the particular skills that services have developed; and to value them.

So for example the pre-treatment approach that Jay Levy has described, which is all about getting where this individual client is at, was specifically tailored to the homelessness world. Levy's work and approach is an example of a thoroughly person-centred approach, being very careful about engagement, forming a relationship with somebody who is quite possibly going to be initially fairly distrustful, or at least wary. For a more over-arching theoretical orientation, humanistic psychology is once again particularly useful here, but now particularly for the stress on relationships, on starting to engage and recover.

The other main psychologies that are likely to be helpful are those related to understanding behaviour in terms of trauma and adverse childhood experiences, predisposing any one individual to later vulnerability. Equally useful will be those techniques with their roots in psychological therapies of all kinds – behavioural, attachment-based, even at time the medico-diagnostic models; at least a modicum of awareness of some of these approaches will be useful, if only to know when to enlist more specialist help.

NB: It's particularly easy to make a case for the vulnerabilities thesis in the case of a more specialist support service intended for a particular group, such working specifically with people who come through the mental health services, or care leavers, refuges and supports for women - or anybody - escaping domestic violence; arguably services for ex-offenders should be seen as working with a quite particular vulnerability.

But the key thing is: when the issue is around personal vulnerability, you don't necessarily know in advance what this person's life experience has been - what things there may be lurking in their history and their biography. So you have to have the skills and the processes ready to engage, to effectively engage anybody and to identify and tease out what it is in particular they need.

You might also want to be deliberately addressing the working social structure of your organisation, the opportunities to engage that you can offer, and the kind of things that you can get people involved with. So you might develop occupational or social therapy, creating a set of roles that allow people to grow into a new role or a new status - things like peer mentoring, and being on service user scrutiny board, or whatever form of co-production suits the service. In this way the skills of engagement that Jay Levy has talked about, which we've described as being central to developing a psychologically informed environment, can be written into the whole service offer so that the whole environment helps you in encouraging developing engagement.

So that, in short, is the psychology implied in vulnerability thesis, as applied in the homelessness sector.

Psychology in the Swiss Cheese model

Rather than the macro-social world of sweeping economic forces, or the micro-social worlds of highly personal individuals' needs, the Swiss Cheese model instead draws our attention to the meso-social world of services and service eco-systems. In terms of both initial and long-term engagement with a potential service user, the key issue implied in the Swiss cheese model is that services need flexibility, and the local eco-systems of services needs coherence.

It seems clearly the case that all services gain from being as person-centred as they can manage, and in the Swiss cheese model, this has to be at a premium. This then has clear implications for the management of services; and for the mindset and values of managers, to aim for flexibility in dealings with individuals.

But achieving this flexibility in practice is not simply the preserve of any one or even of many services. It suggests a need for closer co-operation with other agencies in the locality, to address gaps in systems and pathways. Managers of services can be at the forefront of this process, helping to identify gaps as they are experienced by the users and staff of their services, and considering how they might enhance sector engagement, to tackle those issues.

But as for the psychology required here, if system coherence and gaps are the key factors at play, the need to address all the potential emotional meanings of homelessness for the individual is dwarfed by the need not for individual psychology, but for social and organisational psychology.

Funding and other systemic issues

To hear and take on board this service-led feedback requires addressing the way that services are provided and funded; and that in turn means addressing the mindset of commissioners and funders. Here we come up against the dominant paradigm for public goods delivery over the past 20 to 30 years, which is the model known as the New Public Management, or NPM.

Sometimes identified as 'the purchaser/provider split', or more broadly as the political philosophy 'neo-liberalism', NPM is in fact based not just in a narrowly 'value for money' view of services, but also on an underlying psychology that is rarely exposed to question. In essence, it is the view that public sector 'providers' are just like any other economic agents, and motivated solely by financial reward. The underlying belief about human nature in NPM is that all humans, even those in public and welfare services and charities, are in fact led by 'extrinsic motivation' – that they must be paid to do the right thing; and others must decide what that is.

A challenge to the view that philanthropic services were entirely and single-mindedly philanthropic was arguably quite refreshing, when it was first proposed by critics who noted the growth in white collar and professional jobs that were created, absorbing a large slice of the budget intended for the poor and vulnerable. But it was increasing adopted and co-opted by others with a far more punitive view of the supposed dependency culture that welfare created.

By the turn of the 21st century, the hegemony of the NPM as the way to manage and even to 'drive improvement' in services was almost complete. If we are now to reverse this trend, and to propose instead that the experience of 'providers' can be trusted, we also need mechanisms by which these views can be heard; and this is one gap that we hope the Pizazz and the PIE Abacus may be able to help to fill.

NB: This preference for quantifiable 'outcomes' is matched and exacerbated by another contemporary 'philosophy of value' that compounds the NPM's distrust of service providers' own views with a demand for 'evidence-based practice'. This however gives preferential advantage to 'practices' that lend themselves to standards of evidence based on the laboratory test as the 'gold standard'.

This model of objective external verification is arguably well suited to some intrusive medical procedures such a surgery, in which the characteristics of the individual patient are only marginally relevant; and besides, the patient is passive, often anaesthetised, and not expected to co-operate let alone participate in their own healing. It is also well suited – and most needed – in tests of commercially developed pharmaceuticals, where these private sector companies, accountable to share-holders, may indeed be as 'extrinsically motivated' and self-serving as the NPM model assumes.

But this model of evidence is quite inappropriate for complex interventions for complex needs, where the more complex evidence paradigms of public health are better suited; let alone to person-centred services, where every successful outcome may need to be quite different. The example of social prescribing is relevant here.

In mental health services, social prescribing - that is, activity- and participation-based options, very often within a supportive environment and a community ethos - had struggled for some years to demonstrate a clear 'evidence base' for their effectiveness, as compared with medications, or manualised and supposedly standardised treatments such as CBT. But as soon as GPs were able to prescribe with flexibility, using their trusted judgement in discussion with their patients, we have seen a huge growth in take up.

Back to the front: psychology within the services

We can now return to the question of the individual psychology that we might find useful, in the swiss cheese account of homelessness. What can be said about the 'psychology' needed within services, to respond effectively in the swiss cheese world? And how do we create more psychologically informed services, in this account?

Firstly, one clear point is that there will be no one psychological model that fits all services. (This is another reason why there is no one 'right' way to be a PIE, and to respond to such a range of needs.) At service planning level, there will need to be both a multiplicity and a wide range of services – as there typically is. Between them each of these may be focussed to pick up their service users at various key points anywhere across the entire range of routes into homelessness, and with different degrees of 'entrenched-ness' or 'chronicity'.

Secondly, achieving the flexibility in responsiveness that the Swiss cheese model implies requires that when a person arrives at or comes to the attention of any service, you may have to be completely open-minded as to what the person's previous history has been before they arrived in the service. With the Swiss cheese model, you really don't know how many nets, or holes in the net, the person has fallen through before coming to the service,. Even when somebody appears vulnerable, you don't know how far back that vulnerability may go; or what strengths they may have, that they were unable to access.

The practical implication is that at systems level your services should not be presupposing vulnerability or emphasising support needs in the way that a treatment services will do. In any specific service, some form of triage would often be better than a blanket policy; but you may want to have specialist support available, as need be. Co-working and even co-location are often particularly valuable for such a variety of needs for this totally disparate client group, and/or a 'no wrong door' philosophy. You might want to have very good links with other agencies that you can either bring in, or refer people on to, with reasonably good confidence that your own prior assessment will carry some weight.

People don't typically want to be repeating their story to every worker that they encounter, as they move through a range of services; and they most would prefer things were a more joined up. One clear finding though is the at forming a trusting relationship for many is not easy, and once that trust has been achieved, it is quite un-helpful to commission what has been termed a staircase of services, each requiring the 'user' to start afresh. Continuity may be hard to build in; but where it can, it is valuable. .

Nevertheless, the counterpoint to this is that services should not assume that everyone is in need of a long-term support. You might well be the first person to really engage this person, but equally, your service may be one of many that they've been through, and you're not necessarily the centre of their world. You are just a part of their trajectory through life, and although it's important that you play your role in a constructive way as possible, you don't want to be hanging on to that individual for any longer than you need to.

That would be particularly true of youth services, where youth is naturally a period of transience and people will definitely move on. Although, of course, young people who find themselves homeless will often have fallen through particular family nets and your service may be the first substitute family or peer group that they properly feel safe with. So working out exactly how to get that balance right is quite a sophisticated task.

You do really want to be engaging with other community support, so identifying pathways through your service and identifying ways in which you can work with other agencies. And that's part of trying to get a better joined up service, so there are fewer gaps in the nets. And when people do fall through the nets they can bounce back out faster.

Thirdly, in this model, for any one individual falling through and being unable to bounce back may be quite legitimately experienced as much as a matter individual bad luck as it is to do with systemic failures. We must then be aware that people may respond to their own luck, good or bad, in very different way, from self-blame to rage at the system. Some will settle for where they are at (quite literally) and some will espouse, even romanticise. For many perhaps there will be an element of both.

What is more, the balance in their relative ease with their current circumstances may shift over time, and in specific conversations one version or another comes to the fore. To allow services to engage and build on 'where they are at', a narrative therapy approach that works with the storied that people tell themselves may be particularly useful.

For the client, having fallen through the safety nets you thought might be there, it may feel that it was just bad luck on your part; you didn't get the breaks. Or you may feel rather aggrieved; life is not fair, and you got the raw deal. You may feel that you're the victim, or equally that you're the architect of your own bad luck. You might, in different moods, feel all of these reactions. There may be all kinds of complex ambivalences around in the Swiss cheese model, that services need to address. One thing we can particularly say is that you don't want to necessarily stress people's deficits just because somehow they've fallen through, just through an unlucky roll of the dice.

There is still an economic case that can be made for better communications between agencies for more efficient referral and for better engagement when somebody does come through to you. But in particular I think the responsibility of services will be to inform commissioners and to inform other agencies of where the gaps and where the barriers are. You may have to be prepared to go that extra mile and help fill in those gaps with your own staff and your own time, because until the gap is closed, you are the person holding the holding the baby.

So a little extra flexibility perhaps on behalf of the services is called for, using this Swiss cheese model. But certainly liaising with other agencies, getting better referral mechanisms in and out of your service, is important. Also more effective co-working, whilst individuals are in any one service. Those are all key areas that the Swiss cheese model would suggest we should look at.

Overall, we may say that the further any service can go – and is allowed to go, by virtue of the funding and outcomes set by their funders – and the more person-centred the service can be, the better able to respond to the unpredictability of each individual trajectory.

Psychology across the range in the homelessness sector

So we have our three different models, all making different demands on the homelessness services in wanting to react appropriately to the needs of each actual individual.

So to sum up: the central issue in the economic model is it can happen to anyone: Let's get them out of there as fast and as far as possible. The central issue in vulnerability is something like 'a stitch in time' - if you can catch that person and meet their needs, you stop them falling through further nets, but you do need to be there for them. And the central issue in the Swiss cheese model is perhaps as much around working better together. It is certainly much the same 'stitch in time', but here it's as much around issues of working with the gaps and working with the pathways in, and out and through services.

But whilst some services may be positioned to encounter and deal primarily with one part of another of this range, and the personal, emotional and psychological difficulties they may find there. The sector as a whole needs to cover all these bases; but it's my contention that all services must cultivate the versatility to respond to the next person that walks in the door.

Whichever model we might give precedence to, the underlying message is that all of them have some validity; and reconciling them all in each situation, dealing with the emotional issues is complicated work; and services need to recognise this in considering the support needs of staff.

***

Post script: Managing contradictory messages

It is the first two of these models that will tend to be uppermost in the understanding of the general public, and what they expect from homelessness services. The third is an issue more for the service providers and commissioners, and the way these issues are presented can be tricky to explain to those who do not think through the issues.

Yet for managers of these services, these systemic issues and problematic service boundaries may be an issue of some concern – especially where the staff of any one service increasingly find themselves under pressure to accept referrals that place demands on their service, and their workers, that go beyond their original brief and training; or where they are forced to keep someone on their books, and occupying a space, simply because the move-on services are lacking.

The conflicts that arise for individual workers in attempting to reconcile multiple issues and sometimes contradictory expectations have been explored by sociologists working in the field of role theory. The thesis first proposed by Mervyn Lipsky was that services agencies are often bearing a burden of contradictory expectations and principles, and it is often the individual worker who then, in day-to-day dealings with their clients, must manage the clash.

Lipsky called these workers 'street level bureaucrats', and there have been some attempts more recently to understand the inner conflict of individuals who are torn between contradictory impulses and pressures. Within the health service there has been more concern at the wear and tear on staff not just of general exhaustion, but of 'moral distress', by which is meant the anguish felt by a worker at not being able to provide what they feel they ought to be able to provide

In an article first published in Human Relations (2006), and re-published on the PIElink (with the permission of the author), Paul Hoggett offers a rich and sympathetic picture of the emotional wear-and tear of moral conflicts entailed in working with those with challenging behaviour in areas of public concern. Hoggett argues that:

'...the public sphere is the site for the continuous contestation of public purposes and this means that questions regarding values and policies saturate all public organisations, particularly at the point of delivery. Public organisations have to contain much of what is disowned by the society in which they are situated.

'It follows that the fate of the public official, sometimes referred to as the 'street-level bureaucrat', is to have to contain the unresolved (and often partially suppressed) value conflicts and moral ambivalence of society...'

Hoggett's thinking comes from an evolving tradition that deliberately fuses psychodynamic insights and social systems analysis. When considering how best to support staff with the dilemmas that can arise in work with complex needs, it may be helpful to recognise that there really are contradictory expectations on what a welfare service should be doing, and how. Striking a balance is genuinely hard, and stressful. A space to acknowledge and share that may be the best support we can find.

On the PIElink there is also now a brief excerpt from one of the forums of 2023, in which I give a very brief account of another insight from family therapy, an almost forgotten approach called 'furore theory'. Both Hoggett's writings, and those of the theorist of furore theory whose name is now lost, deserve to be better known.

CHAPTER 4

TRAUMA IS NOT THE ONLY PSYCHOLOGY: ADVERSE CHILDHOOD EXPERIENCES AND THE DEVELOPMENT OF RESPONSIVE SERVICES

Note that this essay is the first of several here that were in preparation for publications but then stalled. This was written with a structured abstract and full references, which are embedded in the text in the manner of more orthodox journal-published papers. Here, for publication in this book, the abstract is retained and included, as it still functions as a handy brief introduction to the subject.

But the references in the text do not now go to a references section at the end of the paper. Instead, the references are on the matching page on the PIElink website. This allows the reader to go with one click to all the pages and items in the Library that would otherwise have appeared in the references section, with lengthy URLs; and this means we can link to audio and video; and to up-date this material as it develops.

NB: All references here identified as 'PL, n.d.' refer to pages of the PIELink community of practice website, www.pielink.net. (The 'n.d.' here is journal style for 'no date', used for websites.)

Abstract

There is growing recognition of the significance of psychological and emotional trauma, and the long shadow that it may cast on the future life of those who have been exposed to traumatic events – and especially to the longer-term and deeper damage of prolonged exposure.

This recognition has given rise to a new approach, known as Trauma Informed Care (TIC), which stresses and encourages an awareness of trauma as a root cause of current difficulties for many with 'complex needs'. TIC motivates and points the way towards better responses from staff and services.

Yet some services report a difficulty in stepping up a gear from trauma awareness in staff to actual changes in the policies and procedures of the agencies attempting to meet these needs, even with this new understanding.

In this paper, we begin by exploring the ways in which one model of the long-term impact of early psychological trauma, known as ACES (for Adverse Childhood Experiences), can be translated into actual working practice in services.

This translation from theory to practice is effected using a service development framework now current in the UK, which aims to develop what are known as Psychologically Informed Environments, or PIEs.

We then explore some of the evidence for a wider range of psychological, social economic and political issues that such service environments must also take into consideration.

We suggest that in fact, many services in practice actually do so; but they must now perhaps articulate this greater breadth of perspective more clearly, for their real strengths to be better appreciated.

* * *

ACEs as a psychological model for services' practice

Adverse childhood experiences (ACEs) have been defined as stressful or traumatic events in early life, including abuse and neglect, whether physical or sexual; and household dysfunction such as witnessing domestic violence or growing up with family members who have substance use disorders, or a history of incarcerations. (Public Health Scotland, n.d.; SAMHSA, n.d.)

Research shows that such ACEs are strongly associated with the development and prevalence of a wide range of health problems throughout a person's lifespan, a significant risk factor for substance use disorders, and can also impact negatively on their acceptance of prevention efforts (Nanni et al 2011).

ACEs research therefore provides a well-validated psychological understanding to help to interpret dysfunctional behaviour that many services might draw upon, where its insights suit the client group and the setting in which the service works. It may for example be especially helpful in shedding light on a pervasive distrust or rejection of offers of support from care or authority figures – the reactions that have sometimes been characterised as 'flight, flight, freeze or fawn'..

Yet with such a wide range of possible subsequent manifestations in troubled lives, and with the additional complications of co-morbidity, and of the effects of self-medication with alcohol or drugs, translating the insights from research into effective conclusions for practice has sometimes proven problematic. For the 'helping professions', this research is affirmative, and suggests constructive treatment approaches for those that do engage; but it is rather less so for non-clinical community services such as housing support providers, whose staff are not versed in psychology language, and whose job descriptions may not easily marry up with such sophisticated ideas.

Introducing the Psychologically Informed Environment

As one example of a psychological model, ACEs research and insights nevertheless fits readily into the overall framework for psychologically informed environments (PIEs). This is a way of thinking about homelessness (and other) services' work that has lately gained some traction in the UK. Here, ACEs would be identified as one example – although, as we will later see, still only one among many useful models - of one of the PIE framework's key terms: 'psychological awareness'.

The formulation of what it means to work as a PIE has evolved somewhat over a ten year period, since first proposed (Johnson & Haigh, 2010; Keats et al, 2010; HomelessLink, 2018; Johnson, 2023). Sometimes taken to be a prescription as to what creative services should do, the authors had always argued that it was intended originally as a description of what they are doing – all be it an account that consciously intended to be constructive.

For those not already familiar with the PIEs approach, a brief outline at this point may therefore be useful; and this can then illustrate the way that ACEs research can be translated into operational practice, using this framework.

The most recent attempt to identify the core themes suggests five main (or 'top tier') overall 'themes', each then made up of more specific elements of observable practice, with 'psychological awareness' being one of these core themes. Adoption of any explicit psychological model then falls within the range of practical actions that come under this overall theme.

In the most recent PIEs framework, all these issues in practice are now clustered under five (a.k.a. the 'Big Five') main headings, or 'themes':

- Developing 'Psychological Awareness'
- Emphasising 'Staff Training and support'
- Encouraging' Learning and Enquiry'
- Creating and using' Spaces of opportunity'
- 'Rules, Roles and Responsiveness' (a.k.a 'The Three R's')

In the PIE approach, a psychological model *per se* is defined very broadly as any application of theory - not solely from clinical or research psychology - that helps to increase our understanding, and so enhance our sensitivity and capacity for relationship-building with the populations we serve.

Aiming for as much conceptual economy as was deemed possible granted the variety and complexity of these issues and correspondingly complex services responses, the rest of the PIEs framework then spells out all the issues that a service may then need to consider, when trying to operationalise any particular model (PL[a], n.d.).

Embedding the 'psychological model' in services

So if a service adopts ACEs as its psychological model, it will also want to consider in some detail what more pervasive sensitivity or 'psychological awareness' it would now want to see expressed in practice throughout the whole of the service. It can then work backwards from the model, to identify any specific techniques and approaches that it might want to adopt, in the light of this new, and more specific understanding.

It will then want to look at what training it provides, not just in the broad understanding of ACEs, but in the actual techniques and practices that it wants its staff to use. Recognising now how deeply and tortuously embedded early experiences can be in their impact on present behaviour and reactions, the service will probably also want to give particular thought to the support needs of staff, including volunteers and peer support workers, tackling such issues. (PL[b], n.d.).

It will, for example, very likely want to encourage some form of reflective practice for frontline staff (and others such as volunteers), to embed and infuse this way of understanding into day-to-day practice (PL[c], n.d.). Research is still limited in this field, but early efforts suggest that reflective practice is a particularly effective way of getting frontline staff engaged in approaching users' problems, and organisational change, with greater empathy and enthusiasm (Boobis, 2016, 2017; Middleton and Broadbridge, 2019: PL[d], n.d.).

Any service with ACEs as its psychological model may also want to have user groups to consult with, for their feedback. Being in all probability one of a number of services operating locally, it will want to take advantage of any local forums to discuss and keep abreast of the shifting nature of needs and demands for the local service to adapt as need be.

It will also want to be aware of current research and thinking; and perhaps even contribute to it, working perhaps with local or national researchers. It may well want to keep its developing practice under review, with time out sessions such as awaydays. Overall, to develop the necessary flexibility and resilience of the service, it will want to establish a culture of enquiry, to become truly a learning organisation (Woodcock & Gill, 2013).

All the above activities will then fall under the overall theme of encouraging an attitude of Learning and Enquiry' within the organisation, and in its dealings with others. Within this broader thinking and rethinking, there are nevertheless some issues in more immediate day-to-day practice that will stand out.

The most obvious perhaps will be how the service goes about engaging with service users, actual or potential. The physical spaces are important here – the layout of a building, especially any reception area and any spaces for socialising or for practical tasks where people will interact such as cooking and cleaning, the privacy of individual rooms or more confidential areas. The signage, lighting and colour schemes, even potted plants – all will deserve some thought. (Boex, 2012; Pable, 2015 and other dates: Genesis, 2015; PL[e], n.d.)

Likewise there are less obvious 'spaces' that are created or implied by the pathways into and out from the service – where it fits, in the local network of 'eco-system' of services, and the role it hopes to play in people's lives (Lankelly Chase, 2016; PL[c], n.d.). This may define the service's eligibility criteria, the referral routes and processes, the extent of information sharing and handovers from one team to another; even whether to offer a very temporary and transitional service or a longer term one, with perhaps for some a permanent support presence. From this there may follow questions over whether to provide a discrete and fully confidential service, or to encourage a supportive community of users - the more theoretical understanding of ACE should influence all these practice issues (PL[f], n.d.).

Likewise there may be a range of opportunities created for service users for engagement in the service itself, designed – hopefully – to address the issues that the user or potential user experiences as difficulties, in their own terms (Levy 2014, 2016, 2017; O'Connell et al, 2006; Boland, 2019). There might for example be a user consultation group, but not just for the value of the information that the learning organisation gets from user feedback, but for the atmosphere of user empowerment that it may offer; and also as a valuable and valued role that some individuals may grow into (PL[g], n.d.).

Similarly the service may adopt peer support and mentoring, for example, on psychological grounds, to subvert the rejection of authority figures that, the ACEs insights would suggest, may stem from traumatising early experiences of care figures (Johnson 1981). But peer mentoring and other such user roles can then also provide a valuable – though sometimes challenging – opportunity to develop a new role, turning past adverse experience into strength and credibility (Woodcock & Gill, *op cit*). The scope for post traumatic growth should not be missed.

As ACEs can be outwardly expressed in many different ways, but almost all involving some degree of emotional challenge for staff, there might need to be a range of roles for staff, with a range of specialist skills. There might perhaps be a keyworker system, providing one point of contact for other agencies striving to work with an individual with complex needs; and perhaps offering one individual worker with whom such an individual alienated from services may nevertheless gradually start to rebuild some trust in people, and who can even provide some continuity, as they move on and through other services (Levy, 2013, 2016).

There could be a variety of possible styles of decision-making to consider adopting, from the strict to the permissive, or 'elastic tolerance'. There might be a complex or a deliberately simple hierarchy of authority figures, that is to say, with or without layers of delegation, implementing or interpreting the day-to-day rules of the organisation with greater or lesser flexibility or consistency, in order to suit the particular needs and/or strengths of the particular individual, or of the user group as a community (Johnson, 1981; DCLG & NMHDU, 2010; Gardiner, 2012).

These and other such operational practices, the day-to-day rules of the service, will need to be thought through –

everything from the opening hours to the ways of managing untoward incidents, the timing of support planning sessions or the permission to use particular areas of the building or facilities, the terms of a tenancy or licence to occupy, and whether to expect or encourage participation in groups, or compliance with programmes.

For example, the service might deliberately exclude compliance as a requirement of eligibility, as in the Housing First model, arguing that for some, after many years of chronic alienation from care figures and authorities, only freely chosen engagement can hope to succeed (O'Connell et al, 2006; Robbins et al, 2009; Rog et al, 2014; Gousy, 2019; Homeless Link, 2019; Robbins et al, 2009)

Those familiar with the PIEs ideas will recognise in the account above the application in practice of the elements of the framework. All these are plausible operational implications that might be drawn from the ACEs research; and the PIEs framework allows a way to translate these insights and implications into the working practice of any one service, that will follow fairly naturally from the decision to adopts ACEs as the guiding psychological model.

But let's now look at that a little more closely still. It is suggested here that where the ACE model is useful to understand the client group then the rest of the PIEs framework can fit around it, to operationalise and support that model. That 'where' does however imply an element of questioning, to ask just how relevant any one psychological model is to a particular service, a particular client group, and especially, to a particular individual. One of the principles in an assessment of a services as a PIE is that it is important that all staff – including volunteers and users - are able to question how appropriate any chosen psychological model really is, for their particular work (Pizazz handbook, PL, n.d.)

Some cautions over trauma research and practice

The psychology of trauma has lately been taking a central role in our attempts at understanding troubled individuals. So pervasive and so insightful is this model that it has underpinned a development of 'Trauma Informed Care' (TIC) in services such as education and also in homelessness resettlement, and is explicitly commended by many national governments. It is by no means uncommon to find homelessness staff offered quite extensive and sometimes quite in depth presentations on the neuroscience of trauma, and its impact on attachment styles and the challenges of engagement.

This is in large part the result of a great deal or research in neuroscience, in psychodynamic thinking and in anthropology, and especially in the growing recognition of attachment, a theory that spans all three areas, that have all shed new light on developmental psychology (Johnson and Haigh, 2012). Yet the preceding discussion on applying the ACEs model now allows us to look over the value of trauma as one of the key psychological phenomena that underlies much of ACEs research, and the attempt to understand the presentations of individuals after such experiences.

But it is worth noting that recent researchers — actually themselves psychologists — have now found that with any audience or readership, even a highly educated and sophisticate readership, just adding a few pictures of the brain, and a smattering of technical terms such as amygdala or oxytocin, will mean that the reader gives extra credence to the report, as science, even when the use of the images of term is totally gratuitous (Jarrett, 2018). Such is the perhaps rather exaggerated respect that we currently have for neuro-science.

Research psychology gives us further reasons to be a little cautious over the central importance of understanding trauma. All social science students hear, usually early in their training, about the Hawthorne experiments, which suggested that simply paying attention to any group of workers or others can result in some improvement in their performance, irrespective of the actual intervention being studied. Similarly studies of the quite remarkable impact of the placebo effect seem to suggest that when people believe that something will do them good, it actually does do them good (Goldacre, 2006) – especially where the healing-giver themselves has great faith in it.

It is perhaps safest to simply assume that there is some element of this at play, when services adopt a trauma-informed stance, and improved outcomes are to some extent the result of this enthusiasm. But this is not to decry the adoption of anything that improves staff morale. If anything, we might say that it is simply a necessary corrective to the mutual alienation and 'therapeutic nihilism' that in the past had so often infused work with the most disadvantaged and excluded (Dept. Health, 2003). If so, it perhaps simply evens the score, and allows some room for new, more enlightened approaches to come in.

So perhaps the most valuable impact of the recognition of the role of trauma may be, not the new knowledge, but the way that the concept of trauma in itself changes the nature of the discussion, from asking 'what's wrong with you?' to asking 'what's happened to you?" (Eastlund, 2017). As we have seen with Trauma Informed Care, it is that second question that then allows in all the other implicit understandings of the way the world really works, that then means that we can introduce for ourselves, on our own terms, all the many elements of empathy, and of values, that we might wish services to demonstrate (Hopper, Bassuk & Olivet, 2010; Collaborate, 2019).

Other psychology is available

Adverse experiences in childhood are not the only kind of trauma; trauma is not the only kind of psychological model that can inform a PIE; and clinical psychology is not the only kind of understanding that may be needed. Fortunately the breadth of the definition of a 'psychological model' ensures that many kinds of awareness may go into developing services as PIEs.

One useful source of insights into the conflicts and tensions that can surround work with a troubled individual, with conflicts between services, and especially damaging and morale-sapping conflicts within a team, comes from an insight from Transactional Analysis, called there the Drama triangle. Here, relationships can rapidly polarise into a 3-way split between roles, with individual or whole teams then cast as the victim, the rescuer and the persecutor (Karpman, 1968; Berne, 1975)

Although some individuals may be particularly prone to this dynamic, and/or adept at evoking it – and often it is the client that is finally accused – it is a phenomenon that seems to occur readily in all systems, and very common in care settings (King, 2012). But to un-pick this, it is organisational and group psychology that we need to understand, rather than necessarily locating all the origins in the early childhood of the client.

There has been increasing awareness and concern in recent years in homelessness circles over the remarkable high levels of Traumatic (or 'acquired') Brain Injury (Andrews, 2018). This refers to recent and entirely physical damage to the brain, rather than long-standing emotional damage, although it appears that the consequences, in subsequent cognitive difficulties and behaviour, can be very similar.

Here, the research that is probably most helpful is from neuroscience, which indicates that recovery from brain injury is nevertheless possible, as a result of the brain's plasticity; and that recovery is enhanced if the individual is in a suitably stimulating environment. (Hamm et al, 1996; Schwartz and Begley, 2002; Doidge, 2007; Döbrössy & Dunnett, 2008; Cristofori I, & Grafman J, 2017). Whether neuroscience may be classified as psychology is a moot point; and it need not concern us here.

Another area of growing concern has been the number of homeless people who may be on the autistic spectrum; services may need to be equipped to recognise and appreciate the particular sensitivities and the sense of security that those on the spectrum may experience (Drezner, 2017; Churchard et al, 2018). There are comparable concerns over un-diagnosed borderline learning difficulties or other maladaptive learning (Johnson, 2012) in the criminal justice system.

Similarly with the psychological effects of addiction. Until recently, the principal addictions found in homelessness had tended to be those in alcohol; and until the last decades of the 20th Century, move on accommodation after homelessness was often to abstinence-based shared housing, after considerable lobbying from the alcohol recovery community (Conolly & Yaswinski, 2016; Grand, 2016). In the present day, however, poly-drug use is becoming more common, with individuals in extremis seemingly taking any route to oblivion that there may be around.

It is not clear to what extent, if any, group support and re-enforcement of abstinence, such as we had found helpful in the alcohol abuse community, has the same relevance here. Nevertheless, it is shared housing in recovery communities that appears to be currently one of the fastest-growing areas of practice in the United States, where it has been endorsed by the US government as a necessary adjunct to Housing First policies (Malone et al, 2014: HUD, 2016 & 2022)

More recently still, it has been suggested that the psychology and neuroscience of addiction applies also to gambling and other forms of licensed risk-taking, such as computer gaming, with growing awareness that such psycho-neurological addictions seem to use learning processes comparable to those by which ACEs develop, though less overtly pathological.

Recently, at the fulcrum point between anthropology and neuroscience, we have seen arguments that such risk-taking behaviour is more likely in societies that are marked by higher levels of income inequality (Wilkinson & Pickett, 2014; Lende & Downey, 2016). Early trauma and ACEs may well add to the vulnerability; but it seems these dynamics are independently powerful.

Wider frames

The recognition of income inequality also helps to highlight the more pervasive issue of culture, and the still broader role of a community's values, which impact not just objectively on the life chances of all members, but also subjectively, on how they are then experienced.

For example, more paternalistic and/or caring societies, such as we see generally in Europe and in the European social model, tend to see society and government as having a major role is averting dysfunctional behaviour and preventing, for example, homelessness. By contrast more libertarian and/or callous societies, such as in many parts of the US and elsewhere, may see the failing as lying solely with the individual (Johnson, 2017b). It has been argued that when the excluded individuals then internalise these values and beliefs, they will blame themselves for failure, seeing it as a personal indictment, and in effect deserved – with consequent negative effects on their self-image and resilience (Wilkinson, 2017).

How people feel about themselves in the here and now impacts on how they behave, and how they might react to the offer of help, as well as to other challenges. Whether they see themselves as vulnerable, or as outsiders, or as rebels – it's not clear that these self-images and social roles simply stem from early experiences. Modern social theory sees these as part of a repertoire of 'symbolic interaction' that is constitutive of all society, and 'socially constructed'. In the contested field of social causation, such issues are quite political, because life is, and people are.

Psychology in the English-speaking world has tended to shy away from addressing issues of power and inequality, though with some notable exceptions (Macintyre, 2017; Johnstone, Boyle et al, 2017, Williamson, 2017). Continental psychology, by contrast, has often been more willing to acknowledge the dynamics of power relationships as pervasive, and therefore as an issue that services simply have to acknowledge, for fear that otherwise they will simply replicate the power inequalities in society at large (Bourdieu, 1984; Foucault, nd; Lacan, nd).

A middle ground of sorts has nevertheless been developed, in the name of positive psychology, a branch of humanistic psychology with its stress on relationships, meaning and purpose; and in the strengths model, a perspective on many interventions that aims to accentuate the abilities and support the ambitions of service users, in direct contrast to the focus on needs and weaknesses of much clinical psychology (Quinney, 2014, 2017).

Before we leave the impact of government policy, we must include the impact of the dysfunctional rigidity of so many of our care and eligibility systems (SEU, 2004; Lankelly Chase, 2016; Collaborate, 2017). As an unintended consequence, these systems may compel services to pigeon-hole people by eligibility, in order to cost account for funding according to specific programmes of support or care, and/or to conform to efficacy research definitions which will tend to disadvantage or even exclude those with more inconveniently complex multiple needs (Dept of Health, 2011; Hickey & Roberts, 2011; Johnson 2014a, 2014b).

Understanding that calls for organisational rather than clinical psychology; and political or behavioural economics, with the hegemony of the contract culture, government buying into the business model of late capitalism (Parramore, 2018). But there is now a growing recognition that a climate of funding cuts tends to foster short-termism in contracts, with consequently excessive reliance on measurable and immediate outcomes, which are inappropriate for services meeting very entrenched needs (Stacey, 2019; Collaborate, 2019; Spurling, 2019)

At an expert summit (April, 2019) jointly convened by the United Kingdoms' Depart of Health and the Ministry for Housing, Local Government and Communities, to consider the value and the challenges in introducing Trauma Informed Care in the UK, one of the 'take home messages' was that: 'in the UK, you really can't talk about promoting trauma informed care without talking of tackling system rigidities and whole system change.'

Conclusion

The relationship between ACEs (and TIC) and PIEs is in some ways similar to the relationship between Housing First and PIEs (Johnson, 2017a). Both ACEs and HF propose a set of understandings and ways of working which are quite well researched and clearly useful. But to make them effective, services need to draw upon a lot of other, more informal thinking and practice, which is understated and often left implicit, so that these aspects and contexts, though crucial to success, can sometimes be missed.

Through the example of the PIEs framework, we can now see how the implications of ACEs research can be translated into actual, day-to-day working practice in care and support services, in harm minimisation, or even in merely custodial settings. These insights and their implications must nevertheless be 'owned' and customised to the particular settings and the particular presenting problems for particular expressions of ACEs in later life.

This is - along with the heightened quality of engagement brought by active situated dialogue (Middleton: n.d) - is one of the reasons that the PIE framework values action learning just as much as formal training.

Sometimes misconstrued as being itself simply one more model of service delivery alongside others, the PIE framework is not an alternative or rival to these other approaches; rather, it suggests a broader framework of practice in which they can be couched. This framework has therefore been adopted here, to identify and spell out in at least some detail the many features of constructive practice with those with complex needs, arising from adverse childhood experiences.

CHAPTER 5

THE WINDOW OF TOLERANCE, THE DRAMA TRIANGLE AND THE ADJACENT POSSIBLE

In this paper I mean to outline three ideas that each help us to find better responses to some of the behaviour that we do often see in homelessness and in other complex needs services. This is the 'behaviour that challenges the service', as we now describe it, and in combination, as I will suggest, this trio makes for a particularly useful set of insights.

The first, the 'Window of Tolerance', is already fairly well known, as it is often used in Trauma Informed Care training. With its clear and simple image of three zones of accessibility, it is very helpful when trying to understand and work with people's 'behaviour that challenges'. But here I mean to introduce a variant which is possibly not as well known, and a little more sophisticated; but which I find to be more useful still.

The second, the 'Drama Triangle', is probably rather less well known outside of psychotherapy circles; and even here too I intend to introduce a somewhat less well known variant that is very helpful, and - as I will aim to tease out here - also works very well alongside the Window.

The third idea or model, the concept of the 'Adjacent Possible', is probably not known at all; certainly not by this name. But once described it is immediately and quite intuitively recognisable, and quite simple as an approach; and it bridges and builds on the first two. I think it deserves to be given a name, as having a name for anything helps clarify, focus, and share, even to train and support each other, in working with this new tool in the toolbox.

The Window of Tolerance

The Window of Tolerance is shown and probably best known via a useful infographic (fig.1). A good infographic can carry a lot of complex information in a very accessible way, and with a punch; and as a metaphor, is already naturally an image (that of a window).

This diagram alerts us to the emotions underlying a wide range of behaviour that can be otherwise frustrating, disruptive, even threatening; and by helping us to see behind the surface, it helps us to cope, and to respond helpfully. To describe these behaviours, the window identifies them as 'fight/flight' reactions.

Note that this fight/flight concept is quite intelligible, even familiar, as the language of human emotions. But it's actually taken from biology, where it was first identified as a repertoire of survival responses that many animals have and use. The fight/ flight/freeze reaction is common to all animals - even some insects - and it is 'built in', so to speak. For them, as an immediate response of threat, it's not dysfunctional. On the contrary, it is necessary.

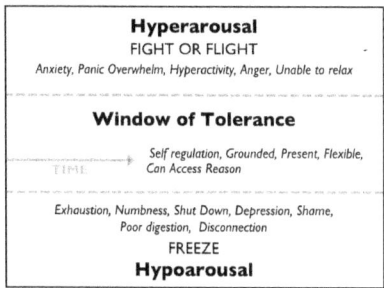

Figure 1

Amongst us humans these same reactions, when they become entrenched, can be, and very often are, presented in terms of the psychology and neuroscience of trauma (as they in fact are here, as indicated in the psychologist's term 'self -regulation').

Certainly these reactions are compatible with the case made by neuroscience for its power in illuminating trauma reactions. But locating this repertoire in a wider, natural and less negative framework avoids the more alarmist tendencies of some early and (arguably) premature neuroscience. For now, let's pause that thought - we'll have reason to come back to that point later.

Recognising under-reaction

One of the things that is particularly helpful in the Window of Tolerance is the way it draws attention to the behaviour of UNDER-reaction, or 'hypo-arousal': poor self-care, apathy, avoidant reactions, perhaps unreliable and inconsistent responses (such as superficial agreement to some suggested course of action which avoids conflict with helper, but isn't followed through - what some now call 'the 'fawn' response.)

We pay more attention on the whole to more actively disruptive behaviour. But we actually see just as much or more of avoidance behaviour - the 'cold cluster' of personality disorder, or in the 'disassociation' as a coping mechanism of some of the autistic spectrum; or just a long history of distrust in authority and care givers. The window gives equal significance to these covert signs of stress, and alerts us when we might not otherwise be looking for such signs.

So far, so good. But then a few years ago I came across a different version of this 'window', which comes with another set of insights in addition; and these can be translated more readily, it seems to me, into constructive ways to respond.

The Window of Tolerance: a 5-band version

Here (fig.2) we see a window with not three bands, but five. As before, we have hyper- and hypo-arousal, and in between, the scope to cope, the state in which others can help the individual deal with some issue. Here is the state that the first version saw as being flexible, 'present', 'grounded'.

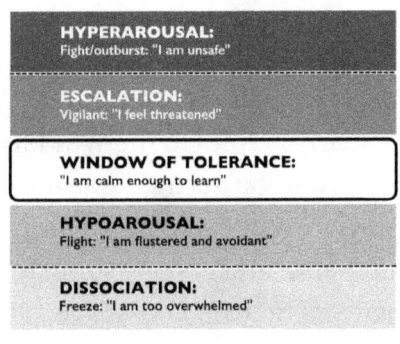

Figure 2

Note that the language here has shifted perspective, from seeing the behaviour from the outside, as something to be interpreted, to focussing more immediately on the inside, the emotion that underlies it. The invitation to empathy here is a little more direct.

That said, I am not sure if I can imagine anyone would actually use the phrase 'I am avoidant'. So there is still a little work left for you to do here, to put this in a more natural language of responses. Similarly if someone is screaming at you, I suspect the phrase 'I am staying calm' may be more immediately helpful than 'I am grounded'. Nevertheless, let's also hold on to that idea of being 'grounded'; it is about to come up again.....

So far, again, so good.

The Drama Triangle

The next concept that I want to introduce is also naturally an image, as it is a spatial metaphor and therefore a visualized one. The Drama Triangle concept came out of Transactional Analysis (TA), and in TA terms, a 'game' is a series of 'transactions' between the 'players'; and these 'games' are like traps that the TA theorists saw people getting stuck in.

The word 'game' though, implies something more dynamic than a trap; these are better seen as gambits – strategies that people use, all be it usually quite unconsciously. Like moves in a competitive game, they aim to put others in an awkward or impossible position. All such games are complementary and reciprocal (it takes two to play, or in this case, three); they all proceed towards a predictable outcome; and all have an ulterior motive or 'pay-off'; that is to say, they are perversely satisfying.

Like all games in TA, the Drama Triangle is a recipe for escalation, frustration and polarisation - except that the Triangle describes a 3-way polarisation of roles (the clue's in the name). The Drama Triangle then suggests we keep a watch out for three typical, even habitual positions which people all-too-easily find themselves implicitly taking up. There is:

- the person who is treated as, or accepts the role of, a **'victim'**

- the person who pressures, coerces or **'persecutes'** the victim

- the person who **'rescues'**, intervenes out of an ostensible wish to help the victim.

In the Drama Triangle, the drama then plays out as follows:

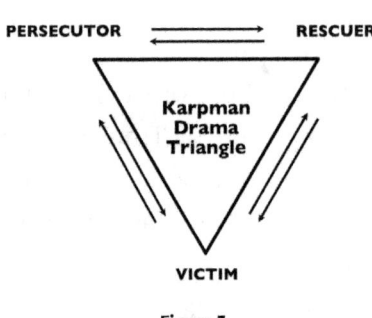

Figure 3

'[Each player starts off] in one of the three main roles: Rescuer, Persecutor, or Victim, with the other principal player ..... in one of the other roles. The Victim is not really as helpless as he feels, the Rescuer is not really helping, and the Persecutor does not really have a valid complaint. Berne, 1975)

Note that the 'game' position of Rescuer, for example, is quite distinct from that of a genuine rescuer in an emergency, such as a firefighter or a lifeguard. When played as a drama role, there is something else going on - something unspoken about the Rescuer's attempts, perhaps a mixed motive or a deep need to be a rescuer, and so they need to have a victim to help. But in fact, Berne says: *'The.... Triangle game inhibits real problem-solving ... [and] creates confusion and distress, not solutions'*.

If that seems a fairly recognizable scenario, there is more to come. One of the most sophisticated aspects of all 'games' in TA is the undertow of complementarity or reciprocity. Part of the grim humour in calling these 'games' is that people take turns; and there is gradually a switch and a subtle reversal of roles between the players. In TA, they call this 'the flip'. (*Thereafter the two players move around the triangle, thus switching roles.*' Berne, 1975)

So as the game progresses, the Rescuer starts to feel exhausted, exploited, and resentful of how little progress the Victim seems to make. They begin to feel themselves a martyr to their work and thankless task; and a weary bitterness, a growing impatience may start to creep in to their encounters. '*Look how hard I am working with no gratitude*,' they might say, if only to themselves. 'A*t least you might appreciate it and not make it too hard – do you have to behave like that? Why aren't you getting better?*' The Rescuer is now feeling a victim themselves, and begins to blame the Victim.

Meanwhile, the Victim too is becoming disillusioned, and starts to complain. Sensing the Rescuer's exhaustion and withdrawal, they may escalate their demands; and eventually even attack him or her for being so useless – '*You're like all the rest*'. The Persecutor, for their part, now feels unjustly set up as 'the bad guy', misunderstood and blamed; and may switch targets, becoming quite scathing over the hapless 'do gooder' attempts of the Rescuer; and so on.

Managing the Drama Triangle

Both Rescuer and Persecutor are struggling with the demands of their self-appointed role; and there is a powerful dynamic of ambivalent emotions that they cannot admit to feeling. Many managers will find this analysis helpful as a way to step back from an escalating difficulty - and also to spot, in the 'flip', a growing energy-sapping ambivalence, from which burn-out may readily stem.

We may often see this conflict brewing within a team, where there are mixed feeling over how best to respond to the behaviour of an individual, especially a service user. The Drama Triangle is understandably very common, almost endemic, in care services. Here the insight is very helpful to the managers of the service, as a way of simply explaining unhelpful repetitive patterns.

Although these roles and gambits are usually acted out between actual individuals, they also appears in conflicts between services, particularly where one is formally in a care or support role, and the other less formally obligated and less inclined to 'go the extra mile'. Where individuals work in teams, and these teams are in different services which may have different responsibilities and values or 'philosophies', we can sometimes find this mutually escalating conflict being fought out between teams, as well as between people.

This means that the Triangle offers a way to understand what is going on that any manager, supervisor, reflective practice lead or therapist will find useful. For most of us, a dawning recognition of the Drama Triangle game's dynamic in play will often start with a question such as: '*How on earth did we get into this again?*'

That is the point when just being aware of the Drama Triangle dynamic can help us then step back and say: '*Hold on – maybe that's what's going on here?*'

But we can go further.

The Winners Triangle

Like many other games in TA, when the game was first identified it was seen simply as a trap to be avoided, perhaps to be pointed out so that others might see it too, and so bring down the temperature at least. In TA theory, the solution was to resist the pull to move into the role that is evoked by the behaviour of the other, and, through reflecting on your own behaviour, to adopt a more neutral, grown-up stance.

If any one individual can then step out of the 'inevitable' escalation sequence, it creates some emotional space, hopefully, for the others to do something different too. But TA is a living, growing body of work, and in the hands of TA therapists eventually approaches emerged with something more constructive to offer than mere abstinence.

In the Winner's Triangle (Choy, 1984), for example, each of the roles of the original Drama Triangle have their equivalent role in a comparable, equally triangular relationship; but the roles of each player take up a more constructive position.

Here the Rescuer now adopts the stance of caring, and listening; the Persecutor aims to be assertive, but without blaming; and the Victim acknowledges that they are vulnerable, but that they do also have some strengths which, with support, can be mobilized towards problem-solving.

Whichever player it may be that first attempts to break out of the role in which they have been cast in this drama - or which they had themselves begun to adopt – now aims to use the same reciprocating 3-way dynamic to bring out the corresponding more positive response from the two others in the triangle.

The strategy suggested now, therefore, is to take and to actively seek the overtly expressed aspects of each position's emotions, and aim to see what is legitimate in each, without over-shooting and slipping into blaming the others, which would, of course, simply perpetuate the game.

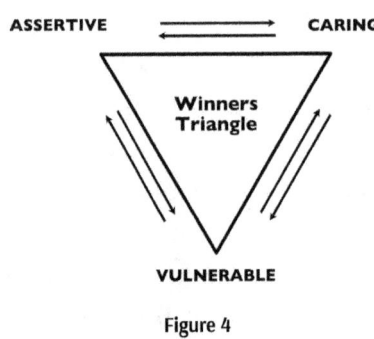

Figure 4

Rather than merely backing off, the Winners' Triangle offers a new direction to go in; and it is one that works with, not against, the emotions in play. It is about authentic assertiveness and self-expression, returned to a more constructive, 'mature' or adult position. (In the original terminology of TA, they are each saying: 'I'm OK, you're OK'.)

In services for people with complex needs and 'behaviour that challenges', we often hear people speak of the importance of being clear on the boundaries in the roles of staff. The Drama Triangle - and better still, the Winners' - perhaps suggests another way to take a stance in relation to overly-dependent (or any other form of challenging) behaviour which is focused more on being clear and centred on what IS appropriate, in role.

It is then not so much a matter of maintaining boundaries - after all, all three Triangle roles are clear on the boundaries they start from, even if they then become more tortured and convoluted under the surface. Rather it is a matter of being balanced or, as the original Window of Tolerance had described it, being 'grounded'.

So this is when we might return to the 5-band version of the Window, armed with this new insight. The intermediate bands, in the 5-band version of the window, are all about mitigating the prospects of escalation into one or other of the threat zones - hyper- or hypo-arousal.

It may be helpful if the person interacting with the individual 'at risk' of escalation can find a position to take and a stance to adopt that puts them, at least, in a balanced role. In breaking with the escalation of the Triangle script, from that may then flow the kinds of responses that help the threatened individual to reciprocate and find their way towards their own more balanced position.

The Adjacent Possible

So far, so good. What, then, is the Adjacent Possible? What is it doing here? How may it help?

The concept of the Adjacent Possible came originally from bio-chemistry, and it comes to psychotherapy, evolutionary biology, macro-economic forecasting, embryology and a host of other uses, by way of systems theory. In other words, it's a very simple idea with a huge range of possible applications.

Even Stuart Kaufman, the professor at a prestigious Californian research institute who first came up with the phrase, confesses rather charmingly that he had been surprised to find just how useful, generalisable and widely relevant, this concept has proved to be. So I need make no apologies for appropriating it here for use in a completely different context again. It is genuinely the same concept, in a new context - although sadly it comes with no simple diagram or image.

In essence, the Adjacent Possible principle states that all viable development, however revolutionary in the long or even medium term, proceeds by small steps, each incrementally building upon each other. Each change changes the environment for each other, and the build up of small changes can snowball into a big change.

The cumulative effect of a myriad small changes, each within reach, may build sequentially into a huge change; and without this possibility, no change would be possible. But each step has to be possible; and what is most possible, in all but a very few instances, is what is immediately reachable, and in that sense 'adjacent' to what was there before.

So here too we have a metaphor using space in its imagery to describe a relationship between states, and a process of change; and let us now apply this image to the intersection of the two previous concepts - the Window of Tolerance and the Drama Triangle.

It should now be fairly clear that the attempt to identify and occupy the intermediate zones between a state of tolerance and coping and a reaction of overwhelming threat is an example of looking for the Adjacent Possible. To expect someone who is in either hyper- or hypo-arousal to be able to transition directly from the escalated position to the coping ground, even with the most supportive and helpful prompting, is almost by definition too much to expect. But the adjacent possible may be in reach.

Attempting, as the Winners Triangle suggests, to offer a position that acknowledges the feeling behind their reaction is attempting to find the ground that is possible. Only from there, and given a little time to settle in - time for the rest of the emotional eco-system to muster, in support - it may then be possible to move to the next zone; which then provides the new state from which the new adjacent possible can grow.

We see something immediately comparable with the Drama Triangle. When we see someone, or some group, becoming enmeshed in this set of conflicted roles, simply to stand back and attempt to 'snap out' may work. But better still is to have a version of these same stances that is congruent with the triangle of emotions, but finds in them something more constructive to work with. Once again, we are looking for the Adjacent Possible.

Again, so far, so good. But if the Window and the Triangle both allow us to see a better position to try to adopt, and the Adjacent Possible alerts us to looking for small shifts, is there anything more?

Possibly.

The Relationship

I would like to suggest that one of the implications of looking for small shifts rather than big leaps might be that it helps us to see the situation, and the people in it, as more fluid, in ways that help to bring out what flexibility there is, however little.

One of the debates in psychology over the nature of personality - and therefore of personality disorder – concerns whether and when particular characteristics might best be seen as 'states' or 'traits'. That is to say, a trait is an abiding characteristic of the individual, whereas a state is a much more temporary response to a particular situation and so by implication changeable, as part of an interaction.

By adopting techniques and approaches that look out for the possibilities of movement, we are by implication hoping that the behaviour we are seeing represents a state; and by hoping that it may be, actively creating some of the necessary conditions for it to be so.

But most of all, by relating to the person in terms of where they are at and what they actually can do, with the emotion acknowledged, this helps at least to build the relationship. Anyone who knows the PIE approach will know that creating constructive relationships is at the heart of being a PIE. If nothing more constructive comes out of the particular interaction, that is at least a step in some other right direction.

* * *

Author's note on 'approaches' in the PIEs framework:

We talk of 'approaches' in the PIEs 2.0 framework, as a middle ground between a more technical 'psychological model' and a broad, but necessary, empathy and emotional availability. The 'Approaches and Techniques' element was introduced in order to allow and encourage staff, managers and trainers to think over what approaches are really best suited to the needs of the user group, granted the role of any particular service in the user's personal journey from struggling to recovery.

So perhaps this 'Adjacent Possible' insight belongs there, as an 'approach' in its own right. Or it might be seen as one of many de-escalation techniques, and/or as part of a harm-minimisation approach. There is really no clear boundary between approaches and techniques, so keeping them together avoids having to decide where they belong.

I'd like to think that this illustrates the flexibility of PIEs 2.0 and its categorisation of practice elements - that these concepts have the mixture of focus and breadth that means we can accommodate most if not all of the issues that arise. Testing that flexibility is where we go, with later chapters here.

CHAPTER 6

ATTACHMENT, TRAUMA AND THE SOCIAL ENVIRONMENT: A BIO-PSYCHO-SOCIAL PERSPECTIVE ON HOMELESSNESS WORK

'Mind, not space, is science's final frontier.'
John Horgan

'The available data, though limited, supports the theory that neuronal growth and enhanced interconnection among neurons ... parallel the experiential and symptomatic changes we witness in psychotherapy.'
Lou Cozolino

Biology in a complex world

When we want to find the most reliable science behind health and therapeutic interventions, it seems that often the first tendency is to turn to biology. Of all the sciences, this is the that is one most closely rooted in physics, which is the dominant scientific paradigm of the 20th Century, and the body is the area where current technologies allow us to explore the subject with relative clarity, objectivity and consistency - the hallmarks of scientific enquiry. We can have confidence therefore in biological explanations.

Until recently, the medical establishment has had a clear and explicit preference for the kinds of study, and thus the kinds of findings, that replicate laboratory condition research: a single, clearly stated issue, a single, tightly specified intervention, with all other factors in the context strictly excluded ('*ceteris paribus*'), and an immediate 'dose/response' that can be clearly measured.

Even public and environmental health - otherwise the most contextualised of all healthcare approaches - takes as its origin story the account of the typhoid pump, the iconic narrative of one man's heroic struggle to win over ignorance and introduce one single intervention to resolve, at a stroke, the single vector of a single disease. By contrast attempts to map the causes of obesity, for example, have offered a picture of daunting complexity (the illustration is on the PIElink).

It is only the growing recognition that the laboratory-based research and evidence paradigms of the 20th Century have failed to translate into programmes to tackle the more pervasive malaises of contemporary society - the 'diseases of affluence' or 'of despair' – that has led to a recent slight softening of this health research attitude.

In this article I propose to explore the application in practice of neuroscience, the most promising contemporary version of the biological explanation. But I will be looking at the application of neuroscience findings in the real world of complex social circumstance: particularly that of homelessness, and the services and agencies aiming to address the marginalisation, social exclusion and trauma that may often underly it.

This may seem a hard nut to crack. Nevertheless I will be suggesting not only that reputable science now confirms that a bio-psycho-social perspective is possible, but that social context, rather than being a confounding factor awkwardly clouding the evidence for the effectiveness of 'proper' interventions, can now be seen as a highly effective intervention in its own right.

Looking for answers

There was a time when the explanation for all disturbed and self-destructive behaviour was thought to lie in the works of the devil. For the mediaeval mind purity, perfection and calm were the heights, and turmoil was associated with the lower rungs of the hierarchy, earthy, and a part of our bestial nature (illustration 2).

In the Enlightenment era, it was reason rather than God that sat at the height of that pinnacle; but still, anything that disturbed reason was seen as a case of a lower nature breaking through. After Darwin that lower order, that animal nature became the monkey in us, the beast. No more need for God or Devil, when Jekyll and Hyde are in all of us.

Since the mid-21st Century and the discovery of DNA, more modern mindsets have concluded that the scientific explanation for behaviour of all kinds must lie in our genes. As recently as 20 years ago, it was not implausible to believe that the mapping of the human genome would soon reveal the underlying blueprint of our lives, of our fundamental characteristics as a species and of our individual personalities. We heard talk of 'the' gene for X, Y or Z - not merely for cancer or Huntingdon's, but also for schizophrenia, for depression, and of course 'the gay gene'.

So widespread and so contagious was the optimism with which this hope was pursued, that some of the vocabulary escaped into popular culture. It is now common to hear people say that this or that belief or loyalty or behaviour 'is in our DNA' - meaning simply 'it's part of what makes us who we are'.

With the mapping of the genome completed, this hope for a single, authoritative 'source code' answer to the age-old question of 'why we are as we are' became untenable. We now know that there are some 20-25,000 genes in the human genome, but the human body is composed of between 50 and 70 trillion individual cells. There are some 30 billion neurons in the cortex of the human brain alone, and potentially a million billion synaptic connections between neurons. There are simply too few genes for there to be any one-to-one correlation between one gene and one characteristic - let alone for highly complex behaviour.

In fact, some of the life forms with the most complex DNA are the seaweeds - the earliest complex creatures on the planet. Being fastened to the land and yet constantly buffeted by the seas and tides, seaweeds need all their versatility to be encoded in their genes, to cope with the variability of their environments. Animals, by contrast, can move around; and many, especially mammals, obtain our variability far more economically, by developing a range of behaviours to respond to our world, with all its threats and opportunities.

The availability of new technologies, in the form of relatively light, even hand-held video cameras, has enabled a development of animal studies in the wild - ethology - that shows just how many behaviours and complex social relationships once thought unique to the human are in fact shared with our animal kin. This versatility and responsiveness in us animals is provided by our neurology.

But it is we, the humans, who have most invested in the art of gaining diversity in our possible behaviour. So malleable is our neurology that we are born with a brain still quite unformed; and it is in our interactions with the world that we must learn how to use it. We are born not just unformed but reaching out, sensing and touching, feeling and trying to make sense of the world.

We are used to associating our 'nerves' with our brains. But sensing and learning is not a specialised function of one tiny part, perched precariously at the very front of the human brain; it pervades every aspect of our being, from our 'gut reactions' to the muscle control and the sheer grace of a sportsman, musician or a dancer.

These observations make the rooting of understanding of our psychology in biology seem all the more convincing. It is no longer so threatening or demeaning to think of ourselves as animals, or to fear the animal in our nature, as once we saw the Freudian Id as necessarily a repository of dark and dangerous forces.

The stage is now set to begin to see disruptive and dysfunctional behaviour as the end result of dysfunctional or disrupted learning, of reaching out and being rebuffed. Like other aspects of our versatility, it is adaptive - but to a hostile environment.

Learning and attachment

Of all the social sciences, developmental psychology in particular has developed a number of key concepts for features of the human psychological repertoire, both cognitive and emotional; and recent neuroscience now seems to confirm that these issues correlate quite closely either to particular aspects of brain anatomy, or to hormonal activity that can now be observed in the brain.

Issues underlying much of human distress and dysfunctional behaviour - issues such as poor emotional self-regulation, impulsivity or risk taking, impaired attachment, empathy or affiliation - these key areas of potential difficulty can now be paired and identified with specific observable brain functions. But what is then most remarkable is how far these problematic areas do largely reflect the language and interpretative frameworks of psychology and its healing wing, psychotherapy. These have developed over a century of clinical experience, professional experience, subjective and often intuitive, which is now given a more confident basis in this 'hard' science.

Of these, perhaps the most significant is the neuroanatomy and biochemistry that underpins what is now commonly known as the attachment system. The pioneering work of John Bowlby first named and drew attention to the importance of attachment for the dependent infant, and explored the problematic consequences in later life if attachment bonds were not securely made in infancy. A central tenet of attachment theory is that early experiences and attachment during infancy then provide the model or foundation for relationships in later life.

Bowlby had trained as a psychoanalyst, but with a difference: he believed that any interpretations of human emotions needed to be founded in empirical observation derived not only from the consulting rooms, but from human biology and the growing body of animal studies. One of the founding fathers of the neuroscience of psychotherapy, Allan Shore has argued that:

'attachment theory has spawned one of the broadest, most profound and creative lines of research in twentieth century psychology' (because it is a theoretical model that can) *'shift back and forth between the psychological and biological levels'.*

This approach has produced a great many useful insights into the nature and variety of the emotional difficulties that may result when secure attachments with care givers are not made, or are disrupted by, for example, neglect or outright abuse. Bowlby's ideas were highly influential in developing our understanding of the crucial importance of parental care. His theories and clinical observations were soon to be strongly backed by experimental evidence, including the use of film - at that stage novel and persuasive.

Bowlby's work was thus among the earliest psychodynamic thinking to be first taken seriously, and then widely accepted, within the mainstream science community. This is in marked contrast to that of Freud and many of Freud's immediate successors, whose exclusively clinic- and practice-based theories and observations lacked the underpinning in more rigorous and empirical biology that has given attachment theory its credence,.

In fairness to Freud, however, it has been the development of film and cameras for unobtrusive observation, unavailable to Freud's generation, that had provided the evidence here, much as the development of video led to the development of NLP some decades later. Sometimes what is dismissed as 'un-scientific' in one era becomes scientific in another, as the technology for observation catches up. This is a point we will return to later.

Learning and neural growth

So central is this new thinking to our developing understanding of how to work with the aftermath of traumatic experience that the prospect of establishing psychotherapeutic thinking and practice with a firm anchoring now in the 'hard sciences' has rejuvenated the confidence of the advocates of 'taking therapies' of all kinds. Much of this development depends upon the opportunity we now have to re-conceptualise personal change in terms of learning and neural connectivity, and with the emotional or 'affective' aspects of learning now firmly connected to the more conceptual or 'cognitive'.

The general principle that learning is enabled and enhanced by biochemical activity in the brain is now well evidenced. Moreover, we can see that learning is especially accelerated during sensitive developmental stages. These are most pronounced in infancy and childhood, but this is a capacity constantly possible throughout life.

Moreover, recent studies - principally from studies of rats, whose basic neurology at least matches that of humans - show that the bio-chemistry that supports neural growth (ie. neural connectivity and thus learning) is actually re-kindled in situations of mild to moderate stress. The discovery that such stress actually stimulates the neural growth and hormones associated with learning, whilst excess stress overwhelms and disables this, has provided new grounds for exploring the scope for psychotherapeutic healing.

Psychotherapy and neural growth

The realisation that neural growth is stimulated by mild to moderate stress is discussed by Lou Cozolino, US Professor of Psychology and psychotherapist, in *The Neuroscience of Psychotherapy*, one of the most thoroughly detailed attempts to translate neuroscience's discoveries into psychotherapeutic concepts, and vice versa. Cozolino argues that this helps us understand and appreciate how the re-triggering of anxiety by exposure, re-working past traumatic experience but mediated in the carefully controlled situation of a psychotherapy session, is the key to learning or re-thinking the dysfunctional learning from past experience.

Observing that studies show that rats raised in 'enriched environments' (ie: environments with plenty of stimuli) have both more neurons and more synaptic connections between neurons, Cozolino notes that:

'During periods of stress, changes in the bio-chemical environment of the brain shifts its focus to new learning. Although extreme stress inhibits new learning, mild to moderate stress stimulates neural growth hormones and leads to increased production of cells in brain areas involved in learning... Stressful and dangerous situations alert and prepare the brain to pay attention and learn...' (P.23-4)

Cozolino therefore suggests that psychotherapy should be considered as the human equivalent of such an enriched environment, similarly promoting the development of cognitive, emotional and behavioural abilities, with a carefully calculated dose of stress.

All versions of psychotherapy involve an interchange of ideas and emotions between the therapist and the client, with language as the medium. New narratives are thereby co-produced between therapist and client, and these provide a new template for thoughts, behaviour, and the on-going integration into a new, more conscious and confident self, of previously buried or dissociated emotions. The exposing of the patient to mild or moderate stress in a controlled environment in the process of writing these new narratives, neural growth and healing can be encouraged:

'The power of stress to trigger neural plasticity is a key element in the success of psychotherapy... As opposed to traumatic experiences, the controlled exposure to stress during therapy is a way in which therapists have attempted to harness the interaction of stress and learning in order to change the brain in a manner promoting mental health. As therapists, we work against dissociation to integrate neural networks. Integration is essentially the opposite of the dissociation observed in reaction to trauma' (P.23-4)

Central to this is the inter-personal context of empathic attunement within a safe and structured environment – what Cozolino calls a 'safe emergency' - in which clients can be encouraged to face and tolerate the anxiety of feared experience, memories and thoughts with emotional support.

'*In this process,*' he says, '*neural networks that are normally inhibited become activated and available for inclusion into conscious processing*'. (P.28)

While emphasising that therapeutic relationships can be customised to the particular needs and readiness of the individual in therapy, Cozolino is careful not to suggest that psychodynamic therapy occupies a privileged position in such encounters. Exposure in behavioural therapies, and interventions from a family systems perspective, he suggests, are all equally fine-tuned and focused on the making of such healing linkages in the safe emergency of therapy. Indeed, he has suggested that education and ministry are equally able to use the transformative power of intimacy and language to heal the harm to the attachment system of early maladaptive experiences.

Language and relationships are not 'mere talk', but operate on a biological plane, and wherever applied with care, the mild or moderate stress inherent in creating these 'safe emergencies' can stimulate neural growth and connectivity. A coherent and carefully focused new narrative in any form of therapeutic, educational or pastoral care intervention, can therefore heal biologically, just as medication can, although this is especially the case where carefully co-produced between a care-giver and a patient or 'learner'.

Humans and other environments

Yet if this is the case, the same essential argument must then apply with equal credibility to many other environments and narratives. While a one-to-one relationships may be particularly finely focused, as Cozolinho suggests, group re-enforcement and other social process may be just as effective, at times even more effective, in helping to create and co-produce a new narrative of experience, and can act as a similarly 'enriched environment', as carefully focused as psychotherapy.

Indeed, Allan Shore - as suggested earlier, one of the first to explore the close corroborations between attachment theory and neuroscience - has suggested (Carroll, 2000) that:

'The group - not only the group, but the culture - acts on and via these regulatory principals. But I would suggest that the regulatory effects of groups and cultures are much more powerful than ... the rules that cultures give. These are the ways in which human beings can pick up the emotional communications of others and can send them back out and that capacity is fundamentally affected by the early attachment relationship that is not genetically encoded.

Group processes, social processes all would be acting through these and acting through the limbic system that part of the brain which regulates emotion.'

This feature may be especially significant for those services working with individuals for whom very close and personal relationships may be - from past experience - especially difficult and threatening. The potential importance of the social environment of groups, organisations and institutions of society to exacerbate or heal is therefore critical. Where individuals may have chaotic and deeply charged attitudes to care-givers and figures of authority and power, it may be that the more pervasive and subtle influence of the social environment offers equally significant or even greater opportunities to engage and to encourage healing.

From studies of exclusion in laboratory simulations, it is clear that any group processes can occasion stress, observable for example in fMRI scans. The social environment re-enforces any communication with subtle but powerful cues that go directly to our cognitive-emotional systems. It is not simply a relationship such as counselling and psychotherapy that can give rise to such healing.

If personal growth via mild stress and careful prompting in a safe relationship and environment, can be understood in the context of psychotherapy, it can also be recognised and understood in a night shelter, a women's refuge, or a children's home, even on a psychiatric ward; in animal-assisted therapies, work skills projects, eco-therapy ('greencare'). It may be, in other words, that the influence of a healing social environments is able to go where one-to-one psychotherapeutic relationships cannot.

For those for whom interactions with others are often problematic, and perhaps especially with any authority figures or group pressures, engagement in activities or any new social role undertaken can be an opportunity for mild to moderate, rather than extreme and overwhelming, stress. What is true of psychotherapy with a willing and motivated client in therapy, might be equally true of a hostel resident in the 'pre-contemplative' stage, facing barriers to engagement in some purely practical skills, group activity, or social role.

In those carefully constructed social environments that go by the name of therapeutic communities, milieu therapy, or psychologically informed environments (PIEs), we typically see roles in the community deliberately created to provide opportunities for constructive role taking, with support. Peer mentoring is another role-taking approach in which the easy dichotomy of care giver and vulnerable person may be subverted, with new growth possibilities for both parties.

It is true that we now find psychotherapists, psychologists, counsellors of all kinds holding clinic sessions, and in some cases working as staff, in hostels. There they may be providing training, team support and consultations to staff teams. What studies we do have suggest that if the setting can provide the safety, and provided the therapist can work with person-centred flexibility, and is not afraid to break many of the rules of formal counselling practice, this can be highly effective.

But it also appears that it is as much the impact of such input on the staff team as a whole, the change it allows in the whole working environment that seems to carry the greatest benefit.

The next steps

Many of the most imaginative thinkers who are attempting to recognise the full significance of the plasticity of the brain are now beginning to explore the implications of social context in shaping the wiring of our brains, and therefore shaping our lives. Once again - and typical of the approach that Darwin, Freud and Bowlby launched - it is evolutionary advantage for the species that is seen as the explanatory framework, but now observations of the brain in action are adding to observations from the clinic and the field.

In biology and ethology we needed a sophisticated understanding of habitat and ecology to understand the behaviour of the troupe, colony or family group in their natural habitat. Similarly, to understand the human environment, we need a sophisticated social epidemiology to recognise the social processes that mean that individuals with particular disrupted attachment issues may be likely to find themselves congregated in a particular part of the human jungle, such as a night shelter, hostel or refuge.

But to understand what it is that is or might not then be constructive in enabling those with damaged attachment systems to recover and mend, we will need new observational tools. Although to some extent we can create simulations in laboratory conditions to demonstrate the role of stress in exclusion, it may well be that it is the close observation techniques of ethology and its human equivalents, anthropology and ethnography, that we will now need, to explore these relationships in all their complexity, in real world situations.

The theorists and the practitioners of psychologically informed environments have suggested that a culture of enquiry and reflective practice must be seen as the essential tool, the golden road to developing a more emotionally intelligent way of working, both more empathic and more robust. Time taken in a team to understand what may be happening, and to see what works, may become the frontline workers' crucial contribution not just to running their own services better, but to our developing understanding of trauma and relationships.

In reflective practice, supplemented and focussed by other new tools and techniques, we may be seeing the closest thing we have to a new technology that allows us to do, in understanding complex human needs, what film allowed us to do in ethology.

CHAPTER 7

STRENGTHS, AMBIVALENCE AND PARADOX : GROUPS, ROLE TAKING AND PEER-TO-PEER ACCOUNTABILITY IN A COMMUNITY THERAPEUTIC ENVIRONMENT

This is the second of the essays here that was being prepared for publication, and therefore has already a full structured abstract and some of the intended references. As before, the abstract is retained here, as a handy quick introduction; and the references now appear on the PIElink page that relates to the chapter.

ABSTRACT

Purpose:

This paper explores the emotional significance for participants of a complex and multi-faceted social structure in a community whose principal purpose is recovery from long-standing psychological and emotional difficulties.

The aim here is to bring to view some aspects of the complex inter-locking group structure of this therapeutic community (TC) that are often overlooked in the literature; and consider their possible implications for other contexts.

It begins with a case study of the internal organisation of the Henderson Hospital as a community in the mid 1970s, describing an aspect of the day-to-day running of that otherwise much-analysed hospital that has had relatively little attention in the past.

This is followed by an exploration of these observations with particular reference to the possibilities for taking new roles within the community structures. It then widens this analysis to consider the implications for other 'community therapeutic environments' - that is to say, community environments that may or may not be explicitly 'therapeutic'.

The wider implications for effective engagement, and for present day service's work with chronically avoidant or ambivalent service users, are discussed in the light of the author's subsequent work and research into the psycho-social dynamics of many comparable recovery communities, formal or informal.

Design/methodology/approach:

This essay begins with an eye-witness account of the social world of the Henderson Hospital, the world's best known therapeutic community - and the model for subsequent 'TCs' everywhere - at a particular point in time. The method is that of a case study by a participant observer (hence the use of the first person singular, for authenticity), followed by the author's analysis of the themes arising, and their relevance to present day communities and other social environments for people with complex needs.

Findings:

A complex social structure in a community allows individuals to take on a range of roles, and simultaneously to have, find and to demonstrate both strengths and weaknesses in different aspects of their lives and social/emotional functioning.

When this structure is internally organised and the behaviour of participants is exposed to examination, as in a sophisticated democratic therapeutic community (TC), it can allow a richer variety of ways to engage in the daily life and therapeutic purpose of the community.

It is suggested here that even in a less formally structured or less explicitly therapeutic milieu the same opportunities may nevertheless arise; and the greater focus that we can see in a democratic TC may allow us to look for comparable strengths in peer accountability in such more informal communities.

Originality:

This paper aims to address an aspect of one of the seminal models of a democratic therapeutic community that has received relatively little attention. It is written by an author who has worked since in other comparable fields, but has not kept up with TC discourses. With that proviso, to the best of our knowledge this analysis is entirely original.

Social, practical and research implications:

It would take further research, using the observations here to explore social dynamics and therapeutic benefits, to confirm how valid and useful the insights suggested here may prove to be.

If they are borne out by the experience of other researchers and practitioners, then a greater awareness of the value of complex peer accountability structures, both formal and informal, can readily be translated into more effective practice.

All references refer to the matching page on the PIElink website: www.pielink.net

* * *

Community structures

Discussions of the democratic TC model throughout the 1960s and 70s had tended to focus primarily on the underlying principles in the democratic therapeutic community (DTC) model, as described in 'Community as Doctor', Robert and Rhona Rapaport's influential study of the Henderson: permissiveness, communalism, reality-confrontation, and of course, democracy (Rappoport, 1958; Manning, 1989; Johnson, 1981).

One of the less discussed features of the model as it was practiced at the Henderson (and also, although to a significantly more reduced degree, at Dingleton and other DTCs) has received relatively little attention, either in the literature or in the day-to-day life of the community. This was the nature, and the role or implications, of the inter-locking structure of groups in the patient community.

At the Henderson, for example, there were at least six different kinds of group. Most well known and most discussed was the 'large group' - the daily whole community meeting. This became almost emblematic and iconic of the TC itself; and the literature on TCs frequently discussed and focussed on the management of the group, as the heart of the 'community as doctor' democracy.

In addition to this, all residents (and staff) were assigned to one or another 'small group' - essentially group psychotherapy, with the fairly conventional psychotherapy group size (7 plus or minus 2) and fairly conventional group dynamics, apart from the capacity for particularly explosive outbursts, and the fact that this was NOT seen as the essential therapy, but only as one locus amongst many (Jones, date).

Each resident (and all staff, apart from the medical director and one senior psychotherapist) was also assigned to one or other of the 'work groups' that took practical care of the unit - cooking, cleaning, maintenance, and a newsletter group. This was possible because all the hospital's usual complement of ancillary staff posts - cooks, cleaners, maintenance staff - had been converted into posts for 'social therapists'. This was a role that was not defined by the health service, with therefore no established criteria or qualifications as to who might become one (I myself was one.)

Members of the community were all in-patients, or 'residents'; and there were (at the time I was there) three wards. On each there were regular daily ward group meetings; so in effect each resident (and most members of the nursing staff) was also assigned to a ward group. Each ward also chose an individual - the 'ward rep' - charged with running the ward group, and convening any additional or crisis group, and usually for 'feeding back' to the large group meeting on any events that needed the community's response, as the ward group itself had an ambiguous and at best only limited authority to manage problematic behaviour, as the ethos was that ultimate authority was vested in the whole community, via the large group.

All new residents, for the first few weeks of their stay, were members of a weekly New Residents group; and those preparing for discharge were expected to attend the weekly Leavers group. There was also a weekly group interview process for the next group of applicants to the community; and for those residents who attended, this was yet another group in the programme. Behaviour in these groups was as much subject to challenge as behaviour in any other.

These timetabled groups all met regularly throughout the week. But in addition, whenever there was a disruptive event, an emergency group might be called; and both the ward groups and the large group could be convened. (In theory a task group might also have a crisis and a crisis meeting; but this was usually little different to the ordinary working of the group, except for the therapeutic vocabulary used to manage a disruptive event.)

'Out of hours' disruptions were more commonly dealt with by an emergency (or 'crisis') ward group; and the actions and consequences were fed back, in the morning, to the large group meeting, whether for further comment and action – or not.

Lastly, there were a few individuals elected and tasked by the community as a whole in structured roles, responsible for running the large group meeting itself, and for calling or agreeing additional crisis meetings. This was a very significant level or responsibility, and the group met together, before the large group. Within the social structure they were then a group in their own right. They might include the ward reps in this meeting, or not.

Role-taking opportunities in a community

Each of these groups also had its own internal group structure, with someone responsible for the particular work of the group - all except for the psychotherapy groups, which claimed to be a democracy of equals, although by implication the staff had a distinctive position in the group; and the large group, which might have two, three or four individuals in the leadership role.

All individuals (other than staff) in particular roles were elected by their peers. But the nature and responsibilities in their roles as between the kinds of group. In the 'task' or work groups, for example, there was a foreman role for the person who would decide on the priorities for the day, and who would then do what, in the practical nature of the task.

They also might vary over time. Over the period that I was there, for example, the leadership group shifted gradually – but eventually formally - from a threesome known as the 'Top Three' to later the 'Top Four'. The ward groups, too, had an individual – the 'ward rep' - charged with running the ward group, and convening any additional or crisis group, and usually for feeding back to the Top Three (or Four) and the large group meeting. If a ward community was particularly unstable for a period, the ward's members might decide to share out the workload of responsibility with a deputy, or any other entirely invented structure.

It is perhaps worth pointing out too, that in the Henderson model there was no individual psychotherapy. This is not the case in all democratic TCs - not for example at the Cassell, where the medical doctor Tom Main, was the person who first actually coined the term 'therapeutic community'. There, the community structure was seen as supportive of, but secondary to, the essential therapeutic work (Main, 1980).

The inclusion of individual therapy, mentoring or any other form of one-to-one reflection in a TC is an option, therefore; but one with huge significance for the nature of the inner experience of participation. (Johnson, 1981).

Implications

In any community as complex and intense as the democratic TC, it would be futile to attempt to list, let alone to analyse, all the implications of this inter-locking structure in terms of emotional impact and therapeutic dynamics; and in any case, their impact would vary for each individual.

But that is precisely the point. In this inter-locking structure, there were multiple roles that any individual might take at any point in time, and over the course of their time as a resident. There were many opportunities and many ways that their behaviour might be problematic; and many angles and directions from which they might find themselves confronted. They might at any point in time have strengths in one area, whilst showing great difficulty in another. They might be earning trust, respect and self-respect in one area; and losing it in another.

Whilst taking responsibility for themselves, and at the same time taking responsibility for both peer support and peer confrontation with each other, the actual degree and practical nature of the responsibilities they might take on within the group structure could be highly individual and personalised, allowing personal growth, enacted, realised and seen in a social structure.

In recent years there has been a growing recognition within services, in research and in policy circles, of the importance of autonomy, empowerment, and working with people's 'strengths'. In recent years, for example, homelessness policy in the United States in particular has emphasised choice, and the need for alternative options for choice to be real. (USICH, n.d.; HomelessLink, n.d.)

Despite the efforts of psychotherapists and sociologists in the immediate post-War era, much of the vocabulary of therapy and 'recovery', and most of the research when translated into policy, remains focussed on the individual, both as the recipient, in 1-1 encounters with a therapist of whatever school, and with 'person-centred' services and individual 'outcomes' (Harrison, 2012).

As in much of mental health, in the field of substance abuse and substance abuse services recovery is also seen as something very personalised. Beyond a baseline, which might even be quantifiable – in the case of substance abuse, the number of days without drinking or using; in the case of homelessness, the length of a tenancy sustained – any other characteristics of success and a constructive healthy life may vary widely from individual to individual.

The democratic TC, with its stress on engagement, commitment, mutual accountability and pooled autonomy, may appear at times to be at odds with this individualistic emphasis (Haigh 2013).

Yet in substance abuse in particular, the value of the group is also well recognised, from Alcoholics and Narcotics Anonymous, with support groups and dry or clean households for peer support and mutual accountability (Johnson and Haigh, editors), and clubhouses with their community ethos and their integration of work programmes with therapeutic and social support and housing (*Clubhouse website, n.d.*).

Ambivalence and the strengths paradox

The strengths model is one that has achieved much approval in recent years, both from those services that have adopted it and from the governments and other agencies that endorse and support effective and constructive practice in social work and related fields. A strengths-based approach explores, in a collaborative way, the entire individual's abilities and their circumstances rather than making their failings (or 'deficits') the sole focus of the intervention (Dept of Health and Social Care, 2019)

The strengths paradox may be summed up fairly briefly: what are personal strengths in one area of life may be weaknesses in another. What is a weakness in one area may even harbour the beginnings of new growth and new beginnings. What is a strength in one area may then be an obstacle to progress, and to moving on. We may actually like some of the characteristics that lead us into trouble, as they are satisfying in some other way.

This recognition - usually unconscious - is what may underlie the ambivalence that many people feel about personal change, and their motivation to change. Acknowledging the weakness and personal cost that lies in some personal strengths is then a complex challenge that needs to be fully appreciated, in the round.

The crucial factors that influence the capacity to seek and find opportunities to change are then two: the openings actually available, and the reception of others to approve or discourage, accept or reject, re-enforce or suppress. But we must remember that 'society' is not uniform and homogeneous; instead it consists in a clustering of small pockets of exchange and influence; and - outside of organised crime - the pockets of the socially excluded and marginalised tend to be smaller and their boundaries more defended.

In the social world 'at large', the incoherent influences of others may continue un-checked; but in a carefully structured and integrated community environment, whether explicitly 'therapeutic' or not, these two sides of any characteristic, the strengths and the weaknesses, can be brought into view and appreciated.

An over-looked potential

In the foundational literature of analytic group psychotherapy, a 'work group' is the term given to a group of analysands who are tackling the emotional issues that arise for them in the group situation (Bion, date). The suggestion that a group might be actually working in the vernacular sense of getting a job done, is completely side-lined. The potential is obscured and worse, it may be seen simply as a form of avoidance, rather than a source of potential.

One last comment however is perhaps worth making. At the time that I was there, the findings were beginning to trickle in of 'outcomes studies', measures of success of various treatment modalities; and early research on the fate of former Henderson residents suggested a patchy success rate – disappointing but perhaps not too surprising, granted the nature of the client group.

But to the surprise of the researchers - and to the discomfort of the psychotherapists - it did seem that those that had most involvement in the work groups tended to do best. Those who rose into positions of responsibility in the overall community did not fare any better than any others. I do not know if subsequent research has borne out that early suggestion - TC researchers with access to literature reviews may well know better than I.

But it is also interesting to see that in the slow evolution of the Clubhouses as a peer support and peer governance model, and in the development of eco-therapy and animal assisted therapies, there has been more stress lately on participation in practical activity – in a supportive community.

In the complex social structures of a Clubhouse, campus or village community, what we see is the sheer variety of possible ways on offer for individuals to grow, with peer support, into a new role and a new sense of themselves and their true potential. It may therefore be that for some, at least, this variety of ways is a significant part of what the community therapeutic experience may then be able to offer, to create the 'psychologically informed environment' that is best suited to recovery (Johnson, ibid).

Over the past 50 years, the therapeutic community movement in 'mainstream' mental health services has almost completely disappeared. But over that time, many of the underlying ideas, and much of the same practice, have re-emerged outside of the health service; and most visibly in services for the most marginalised and social excluded, such as in homelessness outreach and resettlement work (Johnson & Haigh, 2010).

Here do not see the large scale communities that were once found in the hospital estate; instead we are finding more modular services specifically created and commissioned for individuals and populations at different stages of their recovery journey. Yet in many of our cities we will find a multiplicity of services either managed by the same local agency, or in networks of like-minded agencies with local authority support.

If the insights suggested here on the dynamics of identity, group structures and peer accountability do have some cogency and wider value, it is in these single or multi-agency local networks that we are likely to see these ideas translating into a better appreciation of the nature of participation, of ambivalence and the paradoxes of personal strengths.

CHAPTER 8

LIVING IN 'TEMPORARY ACCOMMODATION' - IS THERE A ROLE FOR TIC AND PIES?

A briefing on PIEs in 'Temporary Accommodation'

NB: This essay is an extended version of a briefing note on PIEs in the work of TAAGs and the TAAN, with some sections re-worked here, to minimise un-necessary duplication with others in this collection. We can also now include here reference to other essays in this collection, where relevant.

Other references and hyperlinks in the original briefing cannot be included in this, the printed text; but can be found on the corresponding page on PIElink, along with any more recent developments in the work of TAAGs and the TAAN.

The context

As the housing crisis in the United Kingdom and elsewhere deepens, there has been increasing public concern at the plight of a growing number of households with children that find themselves without stable accommodation, and instead housed by the local authorities in what is supposed to be temporary accommodation ('TA'), whilst waiting for more permanent housing to become available.

In the UK, as in many other jurisdictions, families that are deemed homeless have automatic entitlement to priority rehousing by the local authority. They are deemed 'vulnerable' households by virtue of being families with children, without the need to qualify as vulnerable on any further grounds.

One general consequence of the legislation, and of the automatic eligibility of a family as a family without further need to qualify on other grounds, is that the needs of this cohort, including their psychological and emotional needs, may be quite different from those of the rest of the homeless population.

Behind this apparently clear and simple legal position there is scope for ambiguity and local discretion in interpretation. The procedures of allocation of housing may vary from one jurisdiction to another, depending upon the available stock; the process may involve delays; even what counts as being homeless or what counts as a family unit may be a matter of judgement, or involve criteria to fulfil.

The sheer lack of affordable rented accommodation in each local authority area is further compounded by the pressure on local authority budgets and the relative priority compared with other issues the council must tackle; in consequence there is an increasing reliance on poor quality accommodation, plus the disruption of out-of-area placements, which is especially difficult for the children, and for working parents.

Resources and strategies

In an attempt to address these issues at local level, many areas in the UK are now forming a local 'Temporary Accommodation Action Group ' (TAAG) to bring together all involved parties to see what can be improved, and to hear from those in this plight. In the London area there has recently been a significant expansion of TAAGs, with the intention both of identifying the issues and developing better pathways in this area of greatest pressure, and of rolling out the learning to other parts of the city and the country that may soon follow.

There now is a national network of such TAAGs, and a dedicated website (https://www.justlife.org.uk/), with multiple reports, briefings and other information. Meanwhile an All Party Parliamentary Group (APPG) has been created, to share an understanding of all the procedures and policy levers that would be needed to address the complex systemic issues, whilst aiming to avoid the partisan nature of much political discussion aiming to inform any future government.

In addition to providing a local and national arena to discuss ways to improve the pathways to permanent housing for those in temporary accommodation, some of the services in TAAGs are now developing befriending and other social and other supports, specifically geared to encourage engagement, and to maintain social connection and possibilities of participation in constructive activity.

At the first (live streamed) session of the APPG, where the discussion focused on the complex roots to marginalised accommodation, it was issues of housing supply and access that naturally - and quite properly - became the principal focus of participants' concerns. As one participant later put it, this was a broken system, simply not fit for purpose.

Lost in space

Within a complex web of systemic and structural failures that urgently need addressing at strategic level, it is understandable that the psychological and emotional side is not often central in these more strategic forums. It is taken for granted that the situation is stressful, frustrating, even damaging.

Fortunately in these local and national discussions there is nevertheless a concern for the voices of those in this plight to be heard; and from these we can start to glimpse some at least of the issues, and the ways that local services and systems might aim to enhance the sensitivity of the emotional support they can provide.

Homeless families housed in temporary accommodation now form a quite distinctive sub-set of the overall homeless population. But until recently the particular support needs of this group have played relatively little part in the evolving discussions on the development of trauma-informed and psychologically informed environments for those experiencing homelessness.

Nevertheless at a time when there is a growing expectation that services for people in distress should be trauma informed and many homelessness services are finding both Trauma Informed Care (TIC) and the PIE (psychologically informed environments) approach helpful to help embed this awareness, it is worth taking some time here to see what these approaches may offer.

Here we will look at some of the emotions expressed by those in TA; and then lay out the main themes of the TIC and PIE approach, to see how useful they might be – or might be developed to be. But before we do, let us start with a broad overview of what we mean by Temporary Accommodation (TA), who is it used for, and the impact on the lives of those living in TA.

What is 'living in TA' and why is it an issue of concern?

As we have suggested, we are looking here primarily at families, and 'families' may vary widely, so the only broad definition we can use of the population we mean is the one framed and used in the legislation in each jurisdiction. This is what defines the cohort.

Similarly 'accommodation' simply means somewhere to stay; but what then counts as suitable, appropriate or acceptable accommodation is highly variable, it may be partly supply-dependent, and highly value-laden, arguable and contentious. This is the subject of much of the discussion in TAAGs and at the APPG.

But what then does 'temporary' mean, in this context? Outside of the legal definitions of tenancy law and relative insecurity of tenure - which varies from country to country and from time to time - what is 'temporary accommodation', and what does living in temporary accommodation mean, in emotional terms?

For the back-packing globe-trotting traveller, for example, temporary accommodation is where you may sleep tonight, and being transient and up-rooted is part of the growth experience of a gap year. 'Home', by contrast, is somewhere else, to go back to. For the student in digs, temporary may be longer, the length of a short tenancy; but that still fits perfectly with the trajectory of student life, which is itself inherently 'transitional'.

For the long-distance lorry driver, or the sailor, there may be regular accommodation that you nevertheless do not attempt to make a home. For the traveller lifestyle, the gypsy, the home is the open road, the van or caravan, and the life is geared for that. (At the margins, for those that live on the streets some have estimated is that it takes approximately three weeks of sleeping out to become a 'rough sleeper'.)

We should also distinguish here between 'temporary' accommodation and what is called, in the US, 'transitional' accommodation'. By this they mean accommodation – or as they say, 'shelter' - with the explicit intention of providing a route to permanent housing, which will typically include the support to help do so, as part of the package. The nature and the quality of the support on offer may vary widely, but it is typically provided *in situ*, on the premises and easily accessed. Much of the recent work of TIC and of PIEs has been to see how this kind of support can be provided to best effect.

But these exceptions may start to hint at the underlying issue at a more personal level. The reason why we won't consider these other examples as 'temporary accommodation', is that in each of these circumstances, the accommodation is congruent with the lifestyle and life plans of the individual or group. By contrast, what identifies temporary accommodation, as we mean it here, is the way that in temporary accommodation, the individuals in this group can't get on with their life plans, or at least, are severely restricted.

Notwithstanding John Lennon's famous dictum that 'life is what happens while you're making other plans', those in TA, as defined here, are less able to make progress. Their life chances are shrinking. They are at risk of diversion of their life plans into something far less constructive. In each case, this is a waste of potential; and in the longer run, the public purse is the poorer.

The emotional life of temporary accommodation

With so many systemic and structural issues in this complex picture - the lack of resources, the convoluted pathways, limited advocacy channels and policy lever - it becomes easy to lose sight of the individual and their personal experience; and of the emotional support needs of those uprooted and left in suspension.

But when the individuals who are caught up in this way are asked to speak of their experience - as they do, in the TAAGs and APPG - we do get a glimpse of the emotional challenges that they must manage.

One mother housed in B&B accommodation speaks of her concerns for the emotional welfare of her family and in particular for her teenage son, who is unable to invite friends home, being too embarrassed to admit they are homeless.

Another is worried that she may be seen as uncooperative if she rejects offers of permanent accommodation many miles away that will disrupt her son's schooling, or make it impossible for her to get to work and juggle childcare. A parents' evening is a logistical nightmare.

Another - this time the speaker was an individual, not a family - had found himself evicted after a death in the family, and eventually had a breakdown, followed by hospitalisation. He found life in a recovery hostel too stressful, and managed to survive at all only with help from a support worker.

Although surely worry, frustration and anger, sometimes despair, would be quite understandable emotional reactions here, these are not on the whole the emotions and behaviour concerns that we will typically find, and have learned to work with, in other areas in the homelessness sector.

Nor do we particularly expect to find the chaotic behaviour, or the concerns for addiction or similar behaviour that challenges services and then gets the label of 'complex needs'. In short, whatever the quite laudable concern of policy makers for all services to be trauma-informed, until recently the needs of this group had not been given much attention in services promoting trauma informed care. Let us therefore first see what TIC has to offer.

Trauma Informed Care in TA

TIC - like the PIE approach - has evolved somewhat in a continuing dialogue between the researcher theorists and the service practitioners (Hopper et al, 2010a); but usually we identify four key themes:

- a safe and predictable environment
- support personalised to the individual
- a focus on strengths

- gaining a sense of safety and control

NB: in a slightly different formulation - but clearly compatible with the first - the 'Creating Cultures of Trauma-Informed Care' approach to organisational change (Fallot & Harris, 2009) is built on five core values of:

- safety
- trustworthiness
- choice
- collaboration, and
- empowerment

As they say:

"If a program can say that its culture reflects each of these values in each contact, physical setting, relationship, and activity and that this culture is evident in the experiences of staff as well as consumers, then the program's culture is trauma-informed."

It could surely be said that these are sound principles for any service involving human beings. But the TIC authors do make a good case for saying that these elements are particularly important when working with those recovering from trauma, and especially long term, engrained and 'complex trauma'.

In the context of homelessness services, for example, researchers were able to identify trauma as a likely element underlying a range of behaviours that might otherwise be seen as disruptive (Hopper et al, 2010b; Keats et al, 2010) . Often described as 'challenging behaviour', to reframe these as understandable 'challenges for the service' is helpful.

One thing that has arisen from TIC that is particularly valuable is the recognition of the expression of hypo-arousal and well as hyper-arousal – that is, the flight or freeze range of the fight/flight response to threat. From this is derived an infographic, 'the window of tolerance' which can be particularly helpful in suggesting ways that may be acceptable to the individual whose tolerance is impaired. (See 'The Window of Tolerance, the Drama Triangle and the Adjacent Possible', in this essay collection.).

Another useful insight is that these authors take care to distinguish 'trauma-focussed work' - for which more specialist training and supervision is called for - from being simply 'trauma aware'. It is a distinction that is not always observed with as much care as it deserves, and we may need to find ways for staff in services to feel that they are able to respond constructively without crossing the boundary between empathy and therapy.

Nevertheless, it is unarguable that an understanding of such reactions may be helpful at times for many or any services, even those that are not specifically trained for trauma-focussed work, and perhaps this may be helpful especially when the children are struggling, and the parents struggling to cope, just as we will find among families in TA.

TIC clearly therefore has something to offer. It is adaptable and deliverable as a staff training module, and as it is quite generic - also quite well developed in education, where the children should be - it can help to provide a common ground between the otherwise disparate sectors and services of social care, housing and education, and beyond.

Yet in the absence of any particular reason to infer and talk of psychological trauma in any particular case, it is by no means evident that 'the trauma lens' is the most helpful one here, in understanding these families' needs and responding helpfully. Certainly there is great distress and stressfulness in this form of homelessness, but the issues for these families are not necessarily well captured by some of the concepts of TIC – at least in the way that we currently think of trauma, in terms of the neuroscience that underpins much of TIC.

The emotions that we hear of from those now living in TA do not fit too well with the evidence base for early trauma as being the key underlying issue to be addressed. (See 'Three models of the origins of homelessness', earlier in this collection) Such trauma should clearly not be pre-supposed, particularly when there are many stresses and obstacles in 'the here and now' that need attention. The default position here should perhaps be that the complexity lies in the system, not in the individual.

Finally, some services that have had TIC training have found that they had some difficulty translating these general principles, however inspirational, into specific operational changes that they might make in their working practices. Although there has been some very useful work done for example in trauma-informed buildings design for hostels, this is not particularly helpful to services that must house people in any accommodation they can find, and cannot adapt.

Something more tangible is often needed.

Widening the frame

The PIEs framework of ideas and practice is another comparable approach, which many other homelessness services in the UK are finding helpful. 'The PIE' is quite compatible with TIC - and early versions were really very similar to it, to the point where they are often confused. But one of the strengths of the PIE approach is that it is potentially wider in its reach than trauma and TIC, and in recent years, that wider scope has become clearer.

From its original suggestion, the PIEs approach focussed rather more on the holistic nature and context of care, seeing 'the environment' as a working whole; and saw staff training and support as only one element in the whole picture. As we will see later, more recent accounts have broadened considerably what that term 'environment' might encompass, to include the systems and pathways in out and through services as issues to address.

There are also many ways of understanding our fellow humans 'psychologically', and the theorists of PIEs are keen to point out that emotional intelligence and empathy, and the capacity to form constructive, engaging relationships have to underlie all services, and precede any attempts to apply any other ways of thinking or techniques.

There can also be very different perspectives on the place of psychology in services, depending on the version of the routes to and roots of homelessness that we may adopt, each with distinctively differing implications for the way that services might best respond to the human needs that these origins imply. (See for example: 'Three models of the origins of homelessness', in this collection of essays.)

Finally, being concerned with the whole environment, the PIEs approach has been more concerned to explore how the ideas and spirit of the approach can be translated into actual operational practice in a wide range of environments, and embedded throughout a service, including the way the service works with others, to share the learning. This makes the PIE approach, and in particular the more detailed PIEs framework, a useful tool for actual implementation of any chosen psychological model, or other mode of understanding.

The PIEs 2.0 framework in detail:

Although relationships are said to be central to any service working as a PIE, there are then five other core themes, or areas that the latest PIEs framework (known as PIEs 2.0), suggests services might want to look closely at:

- Psychological awareness, to underpin their understanding of the emotional needs of the user group, and also of their own staff.
- Training and support for staff and others, including potentially the wider community and other agencies
- Developing a stance of 'learning and enquiry' in the face of any problems that arise
- Developing 'spaces of opportunity' - working constructively in and with 'environments' of one kind or another
- Attention to 'the Three Rs' – the day-to-day operational rules, roles and the responsiveness of their services.

The PIEs framework: relationships and empathy

Most people, in looking through the PIE lens, tend to start with 'psychological awareness'; and this can then include, where appropriate, any particular techniques for engagement, or any psychological 'model' that may be helpful.

The earliest versions of what makes for a PIE even talked of adopting a 'psychological model', which many then assumed must mean introducing ideas and techniques taken from clinical psychology and therapeutic approaches, such as CBT, humanistic psychology, and trauma-informed care.

By contrast the revised PIEs framework was careful to broaden the concept of the 'psychological' in a PIE, to recognise a much broader emphasis on empathy and emotional intelligence. (See: 'Trauma is not the only psychology', in this collection). So if we can dispense with formal psychological language, and think instead more in terms of empathy and ordinary human understanding, what then are the 'psychological and emotional needs' in TA?

Paramount, in temporary accommodation, seems to be a concern for safety, security; and with that, a sense of being able to have some control over the environment. Safety, as a core issue, is therefore one that IS shared with TIC. Here at least PIEs and TIC are in full accord.

With control over the immediate environment comes the possibility of a sense of having a future, and some scope to work towards it. This seems very much in accord with the issues in living in TA that we had identified earlier, in being suspended and unable to get on with life plans. As in TIC, many PIEs adopt the strengths model as one of their central approaches.

In other homelessness services this is often seen as an issue of 'empowerment' of service users, expressed in an encouragement to active participation in the work of the service, even extending to active user's voice structures, user scrutiny committees, and co-production. In the case of TA, it may not be the specific accommodation service that needs a user's voice, but the relative disorganisation in this 'broken' system that leaves people stranded.

Here the TAAGs do allow these individuals a voice. But the common thread is a concern to feel, and have opportunities to still be, resourceful; perhaps also about preserving one's sense of hope and dignity. (See 'Three models of the origins of homelessness', earlier in this collection) Preserving a the security of sense of still belonging is also not just about having a place – literally – but having a role in society; and we will return to this, in the framework's 'Three Rs'.

The PIEs framework: staff training and support

Of the five core themes in the PIEs framework, the one that usually needs least explanation is the stress on staff training and support. The only two points to add here are: firstly the emphasis on support - the argument that this work is emotionally demanding, and services do need to cater for this: and secondly, that this training and support role can extend beyond the confines of the paid staff of any one service.

Otherwise, several of the techniques and models that we have seen adopted in PIEs have used variants on the pre-treatment approach - described on the PIElink as the core skills of engagement. (See also the next essay in this collection.) Others are less formalised, such as the importance of eye contact; or the use of art, drama, music, photography or sport, to help individuals find a constructive part of themselves.

This training and support can extend to volunteers, to peer support staff, and those actively involved in any kind of tenant participation; and to any colleagues in the local network of services. Simply explaining the work of a service, and the issues they are finding, may itself be a kind of community awareness training that services need to undertake.

In fact, therefore, the kind of learning from talking with each other that we find in the TAAGs is an example of this wider learning support role. Whether we call it training or not, this kind of developing relationships through learning from each other takes us immediately on to the next key theme.

The PIEs 2 framework: learning and enquiry

The third of the 'Big Five' themes is not about the awareness training or support of the staff, but rather it refers to the attitude or culture of the agency itself to any challenges tor constraints that may arise. Here the main expressions of an attitude of learning and enquiry are:

- Making space for reflective practice for the staff, especially at team level
- Encouraging a 'culture of enquiry' rather than one of blame or strict adherence
- Engaging with other local services in needs analysis and service audit to improve local pathways and partnership working.
- Contributing to more general knowledge and development of constructive approach in evidence generating practice.

This is exactly what the TAAGs aim to do. So perhaps the question to explore here is whether the PIE approach can then offer anything to help and support this work. The ambition in the PIEs approach to provide a shared language for all services working with complex needs may be helpful; and TIC also has much the same ambition.

Nevertheless, the PIE approach set out to give a rounded view of ALL the aspects of a service that need to work together to create effective resources for complex needs. Here therefore we might also look at one other possible contribution: using the self-assessment and service development process for PIEs in local networks, to get into the detail.

But before we go on to explore the assessment process for PIEs - with typical humour, this is called the Pizazz - to see how it may help focus on these issues, let us continue, and outline the next of the big themes, that explores the kinds of environments in which we work, and the skills required in different contexts.

The PIEs 2 framework: systems and pathways as 'built environments'

The earliest descriptions of a PIE were largely focussed on describing the work of 'accommodation-based' services - that is, those with buildings that they owned or managed and used as the location for their work. The updated account, PIEs 2.0, considerably expanded this account of the kinds of environments where this thinking seems to be helpful.

On the PIElink website - the principal resource for advice, information and discussion on PIEs - new pages more recently have continued this expansion of the frame of reference, describing for example the work of outreach workers, and others who work in 'environments without buildings of their own'.

In previous work on outreach, we have identified some 'core engagement skills' and a lot of learning to share on the importance of recognising the sense of place and individuals personal boundaries, whether in a hostel, on the streets, or in someone's home, and whether that home is temporary or permanent. (See the next essay in this collection, on Pre-treatment and the importance of these core skills of engagement.)

But in recent years, the original conception of 'the built environment' that is referred to in the literature on PIEs has expanded still further, to include addressing the wider network (or 'eco-system") of services, the pathways in, through and out of a service, and even the commissioning of services. These are all seen as being themselves in effect 'built' environments.

This, of course, is precisely the area that the TAAGs and the APPG are there to focus on. The 'systems and pathways' element in PIEs 2.0 is there precisely so that services and their users can comment on their experience of howe 'joined up' this eco-system is; and where there are gap and barriers to address.

In this way, the original PIE concepts now can in principle extend to any kind of accommodation on any terms, and it should be possible to explore ways in which the full holistic perspective of the framework might be brought to bear on TA. But in the more holistic model that PIEs offers, this is all interwoven with the attitude of learning end enquiry, reflective practice and sector engagement; and with attention to what can actually change.

So now it's time to look at the last of the 'Big Five' themes: how we can aim to maximise what say we do have, and what impact this might have on entangled and dysfunctional systems, by looking at how to bring about change in the day-to-day running, the rules, roles and responsiveness, of services.

The PIEs 2 framework: The Three Rs

One of the most fundamental lessons from the many discussions on the development of PIEs has been a growing recognition of the importance in practice of the constructive relationships that can form in a service: between worker and service user, but also, and perhaps especially, between service users, and between users and the wider community. But just as significant are the relationships between services in any one locality; and this is the focus of the TAAGs.

Those three 'Rs' are the actual 'rules of engagement' in any services or network; the roles that are then available for individuals (and groups); and the overall responsiveness of the service as a whole.

It has been said that in working with and through relationships, the whole PIE framework is needed, for maximum synergy. But in the everyday operations of a service, is it the Three Rs that do the heavy lifting. In the Three Rs, there is the opportunity to focus on what this can mean, in practice, in the day-to-day running of a service.

The 'responsiveness' of a service is in effect the practical outcome of the flexibility that comes with a culture of learning and enquiry; and the responsiveness of a local network of services (see the next section for an explanation) is precisely what the TAAGs aim to improve.

These local networks then try to look in detail at the operating procedures of each service, in hopes to better align them. In PIEs terms, these are 'the rules', and in the final section here on what the PIE framework may have to offer, we will look more closely at how the PIEs assessment and development process, the Pizazz, might be useful to get an overview of where obstacles in the day-to-day running of services may lie, and where opportunities can be identified to make even quite small changes that might lubricate these gears.

Roles in TA and TAAGs

But before we move on to these more systemic issues, let's backtrack for a moment to the skills and the opportunities that ca be found in TA, and ask what, in the Three Rs, are the roles in TA support and in TAAGs, and what is their value?

In terms of awareness of the emotional issues, as we saw earlier, having, finding or making opportunities to be resourceful is important for well-being or recovery. In many other community-based services in the homelessness sector this will include offering or making available constructive activities and opportunities to do new things – to explore and find new strengths, in new roles.

This is often seen in terms of empowerment, and as an example of the strengths model and positive psychology in practice, so that we can locate this in the psychological model that services may be using. It is also an example of ensuring that the mindset of learning and enquiry and any changes and developments in services, are informed by the experiences of service users, and ensuring that

In the case of the TAAGs, making the experience of those in TA central to the discussions is clearly empowering in this way. Many services will work hard to develop or to employ peer support workers, as part of the staff team. Some will develop befriender schemes.

In some ways of working, peer support and the development of a community is one of the key planks of the service's way of working. In some, this is seen as one of the main avenues for therapeutic work; but even services that do not see their work themselves in therapy terms may find the same constructive relationship dynamics being central to recovery. (See 'Strengths, ambivalence and peer support', earlier in this collection.)

In addition, some of the local services being developed specifically for people in TA have been still more pro-active, and created support networks, not just for 'tea and sympathy', but for active participation in sports, walking groups, music, etc. Such practical activity is valuable in offering new opportunities for belonging.

Nevertheless, if the underlying risk here is that the individual family may be simply lost in the complex processes and lengthy waiting times for re-housing, one thing that may be especially valuable is to also have at least one person - preferably more - that you can turn to and talk to. Having someone who knows you, and sees you as a whole person, who can be a witness (furore theory); can even share your frustrations, this can be a life line.

But having at least one person who is not just empathic but resourceful, knowledgeable, and tries to help in whatever way they can, and not just for the parents but also for the children. The role they may play here in someone's life may be as important as any specific task they undertake.

Now what?

If TA and the work of the TAAGs have found themselves on the side lines until now, in discussions over how we can create more psychologically informed services, it may be encouraging to the TAAGs, and the services and individuals involved with them, to find that their work does seem fully comparable with the development of PIEs elsewhere.

But it is still by no means clear, apart from that, if there is any further gain in seeing their work in this light. Though compatible, can we really expect the core framework of ideas and PIEs practice, originally developed primarily for other needs, to be able to help in understanding and responding more effectively to these rather different needs?

If the principle obstacle to progress is the fragmentation of responsibility between services, finding a way to develop as a holistic service may be 'a big ask'. But at this point, it is time to introduce the Pizazz.

Assessing services with the PIEs services audit framework : the 'Pizazz'

In the Pizazz, we have an assessment and development process for services, to judge to what extent they feel they ARE working as a PIE and - more importantly - to help identify where they might make improvements.

The Pizazz is notionally an acronym for the 'PIEs Self Assessment and Services Self-development' process - 'Pizazz' being a show biz term, that means flair, sparkle, dynamism, creativity - and maybe a hint of courage, to stand out, and do something bold. That's because the kind of services we see, and would like to see more of, display all these same characteristics.

The Pizazz is a tool not just for assessing services, but for development, with a carefully structured process, which is cyclical; it can be repeated as many times as is useful, to track progress. It takes any service team discussion through five clearly specified stages:

1. Self-assessment
2. Evidence
3. Analysis (of what helps and what hinders progress)
4. Action planning
5. Peer review

It took some sophistication to produce a process that is that simple. On the PIElink you will even find a page – 'The coffee break Pizazz' - that suggests how it is possible to run through the whole process quite informally in just a few minutes.

But in essence the Pizazz is simply a tool that anyone can use. Like the PIEs framework itself, it's not about specifying a new set of things that a service must do, to 'be a PIE', but rather it's a way to see, and to think through together, what works for you.

One of the features of the Pizazz process that may then be particularly relevant is the suggestion that a fully realised Pizazz assessment - whether for a specific service or agency, or for a whole network - will end with what we have called a 'peer review' stage. This simply means asking some other organisation – one that you trust – to give their own views on your service.

What is potentially most interesting for TAAGs is the suggestion that this can be used not just in a specific team, and/or by all or many services and teams in one agency (to get an overview of services across the whole agency), but in networks of local services, to assess how the network as a whole works.

This means focussing primarily on all the networks and pathways and system coherence elements in the Spaces of Opportunity; and the sector engagement area in the Learning and Enquiry theme. But as the PIEs approach is holistic, it is likely to then draw attention to other areas that will need addressing, to complement and embed any action plans throughout each participating agency, and the work of the commissioners themselves.

There is now a software version of the Pizazz, called the PIE Abacus, which uses the PIEs 2.0 framework to ask questions of a whole agency, or a whole network. This is where the ability to focus on the minutiae of operational practice – the Three Rs – may prove most useful. As software this may be particularly useful for bringing together and pooling a range of views and suggestions from a large number of services whose work may be impacted by the problems in TA, and to feed into the development of better responses.

Certainly some work may need to be done to identify the language of PIEs that is suited to TA, and to the nature of the systems and pathways for this client group. It has even been suggested that a new version of the PIEs framework, a 'PIEs 3', might be needed, to draw more attention to the specific issues in systems and pathways, which can themselves be seen as 'built environments'. But in introducing new models and terms there is a risk of adding complexity and confusion. The more modest alternative is to consider this as an area where the PIEs framework simply needs translating into the particular context where it is applied.

This use of the Pizazz is still at a quite experimental stage, and it would benefit from some initial piloting in a few localities, and a lot of learning from the experience. Nevertheless it seems quite promising, and may prove to be well suited in principle and in practice to the work of TA, and TAAGs. Only time will tell.

In summary

It is at least arguable that in any discussions on the ambition of particular services in the local network to work as PIEs, the TAAGs and their participants can feel that, being on the same page, they at least have grounds for having a say in any service's assessments and action plans, and peer review.

Whether there is any value in the TAAGs themselves undertaking and even leading on an assessment of the network in their area as a 'PIE of pathways' remains to be seen. All the guidance produced so far, and most of the actual worked examples from the initial pilots and since, have been on using the Pizazz within an organisation, or an already tight-knit co-operating network.

Rather than attempting to fit the issues in temporary accommodation into the existing PIEs framework, it might be better to see temporary accommodation as being a test - and as good a test as any - of the versatility of this framework; and whether it may actually help us to spot, value and develop the common ground in core skills and vision, and translate then into new energy for practical improvement.

CHAPTER 9

PRE-TREATMENT AND PIES IN THE MICRO-SOCIAL WORLD

A meeting of minds

When I came across Jay Levy's writings on pre-treatment, way back in 2014, my first thought was: here is a kindred spirit.

It was not just the intelligent compassion in his deeply respectful, person-centred approach. Nor was it just his evident commitment to thinking through, analysing and sharing his ideas on 'what works' - to spell out with just a few key themes where the essential ingredients are in these interactions. This kind of analysis had a lot in common with the approach I had been taking myself, in writing about what works in providing services for this same group. That was one clear thing in common.

Certainly there was a clear difference between our worlds and our work. His focus at that point was primarily on homelessness outreach and assessment, supporting the transition through to permanent housing, working in the spirit of the Housing First approach. My own work, at least until then, had been primarily in accommodation-based support services, and all the stages of resettlement that the Housing First programme had wanted largely to skip over.

Jay's work on pre-treatment is already expanding beyond the realm of homelessness outreach and assessment, and finding validity in many other areas where we must engage people first and foremost on their own terms. Likewise in this essay I will be showing the ways in which the PIEs concept has spread far beyond its original roots in the UK's homelessness 'hostels'.

For the US reader, let me first explain that 'hostel' here does not mean a youth hostel. This is the term we use for what you in the US now call 'interim housing': and the UK has made great efforts over some 30 years to improve the quality of our 'hostels'. My work on 'psychologically informed environments' - PIEs - which reflected my many years working in community mental health and later a scant few as a government adviser, researcher and journal editor, was all a part of that development.

We were also writing in and for different contexts. There were evident differences between the US and the UK: different geography and scale, different institutions, and some different technical terminology for programmes and services. This last, it became clear, is at the root of a lot of miscommunication and the many wasted opportunities to learn from each other. He and I later made this a central issue in a book we then co-edited: *'Cross cultural dialogues on homelessness: From Pre-treatment to Psychologically Informed Environments'*.

Still there was something to this pre-treatment approach that clearly echoed the work we had been developing. These conversations with Jay matched and complemented many other discussions I was having here in the United Kingdom with workers from a host of other services who were, it seems, finding the ideas I had been putting forward equally relevant to their own work.

In fact it would be fair to say that the many conversations I then had with Jay, whether in writing, by phone or video or in person, played no small part in the shift in my own thinking and approach over these past few years.

These conversations all helped to extend the original, more hostels-based PIEs model to cover this far wider range of responses to the challenges of homelessness. In outreach services, in street engagement, in our own (then fairly new) Housing First projects and in a string of other contacts beyond those we had originally had in mind, there was something here that needed bringing out. Still it took some while to tease out just where this common ground lies.

At a conference in 2017 on the research and evidence on PIEs, I had therefore proposed a working party to consider updating the original versions of the PIE. Along with, for example, Housing First, Trauma Informed Care, the strengths model, recovery and a number of other similar developments, I had included pre-treatment in the list of new issues to be encompassed, even though at this time pre-treatment was almost completely unknown, this side of the pond.

What, then, is this common ground, that I was keen to explore?

Common ground

In a chapter in the '*Dialogues*' book I had suggested that Jay's work helped to pinpoint what I came to call the core skills in engagement, those that are needed in any setting, whether in 1-1 work, in street outreach, or in any advice centre, day centre, shelter, or in in-going support to individuals in their own homes. In all the steps on the pathway to settled accommodation, I suggest, these skills will be in play.

In fact even in explicitly therapeutic work, in actual 'treatment', I would argue that these skills are essential. Without that original engagement, no other techniques can get traction. If in the past they have barely been mentioned in the literature of therapy, I suspect this is simply because in explicit therapy, the 'client' is already primed and usually motivated to engage. That primary pre-treatment work had been done, by the client, and now is taken for granted.

If these are the underlying skills, what my own work had done was to look at the wider context in which these individual interactions occur, and how to think through and design these contexts - how to see them as environments that may support or inhibit these interactions, and how to develop the possibilities to be constructive.

We had originally said that any service 'that takes into account the psychological make-up – the thinking, emotions, personalities and past experience – of its participants, in the way it operates' could be described as a psychologically informed service. But these days we have tended to reserve the term for those that did so consciously, for a purpose; and many are doing so with the aim of creating a service 'in the round', as we say in the UK (meaning 'seen from all angles, perspectives or aspects', or 'treated thoroughly with all aspects shown or considered'.

Then we have what we could properly call a psychologically informed environment. In short, many psychologically informed services are providing some of the key ingredients, but it's the PIE that is the whole package. Although if that makes it all sound like something new, more work to do on top of what you already do, what we find is that for many, perhaps most services, it isn't. It's just a way to see the whole thing more clearly – to see it 'in the round'.

Even so, the actual 'environments' in services that we'd had in mind, in those first few years, had been buildings - we talked of 'the built environment and its social spaces', arguing that this must be seen as one of the key components, and not a mere context and an afterthought. In services and buildings that we manage, we can have some control over the design of the building - reception areas, lighting and signage, reserved access areas. We can then, with sufficient awareness, start to develop and design these spaces to best suit the purpose of engagement, the better to meet their needs.

But how, then, can we use that same awareness of the significance and potential use of these spaces for more engaging interactions in environments that we do not own, and cannot control?

Jay's writings had given us some pointers; and these and many other conversations with others then started us off on the trail. It took a while, but I eventually began to see that the key to this was to look at what these spaces mean not to us, but to the other person. These are, after all, the spaces they live in; or those that we hope they will want to.

Incidentally, although we do talk of using 'psychology' in a PIE, this is not restricted to the insights that clinical psychologists, psychotherapists and others may bring to the party, useful though they may often be. Nor is it the psychology of academic and research studies, that see the experience of individuals from the outside, looking in. Instead, we are referring to our attempts to grasp the world as it is experienced, the world-as-it-is-to-them. This is what ethologists, those who study wild animals in their natural habitat, have called their 'Umwelt'.

This goes both wider and deeper than anything therapists will see in their clinics; and it gets to the heart of the common ground between all constructive interventions.

Let's look at a few examples.

Spaces as opportunities

When we approach and enter someone else's personal space, it is important to understand what that space, and the choice of that space, may mean to them. Whether it is a piece of cardboard in a doorway, a tent in the woods, a railway arch, we must start with the assumption that the individual has made their own choice of that space, for reasons with a meaning to them that we must try to appreciate. We will need to show some appreciation and respect for the boundaries we may cross – or be invited to cross. Entering someone's space is a deeply personal action.

There are researchers who have studied the implied messages in physical proximity. The anthropologist Edward T. Hall some years ago had suggested the term 'proxemics' for the study of the meanings of personal space, and how people relate to and negotiate these zones with an implicit understanding. (This is best shown visually; so it's worth looking up some of the videos you will find on the internet. The links at the close of this chapter will take you to a few, to get you started.)

Here I am also reminded of a conversation with a nurse, in a drop-in centre near one of Paris' major railways stations - 'where the ragged people go', as Paul Simon put it. As a nurse, she could change dressings, apply ointments. In her role, she had a licence to touch, permission for intimacy. 'Sometimes', she said to me, 'this may be the only time in days or weeks that they have felt a human touch'. That is just the sensitivity, the awareness that I wanted to recognise.

The same awareness of the importance of boundaries applies, even when they are codified into residency and tenancy rights. As we enter someone's personal space, in their own home - or even just a room in a hostel or a bedspace in a shelter - we can try to appreciate the personal meanings that people invest in that space. However small and insecure, it is populated, so to speak, and 'informed' with the meanings of their own life.

Personalised space

Some years ago an occupational therapist, Leonie Boland, gave a presentation to the annual Pathways conference on a study she had conducted of working to help anchor and enrich the sense of being at home, in your own space at last, for people newly re-housed. Her project involved simply giving a number of residents a camera to take, and later to show, photographs of their homes, of what they had found and what they had done to make it a home.

All the 'personalisation' here was their own doing - but it was the creative idea of the staff support team that had helped them to do it. There was no requirement to put into words what these photographs said about them, and the place - although it might often unlock a conversation. But just to value what they had done, by implication, was sufficient intervention to affirm and enhance this home-making - to bear witness, as Jay has put it.

For another example, there is a drop-in service for street homeless people in the heart of Glasgow, run by the Simon Community. Their approach, and in fact their whole building, had been completely re-modelled after attending a seminar on the PIE approach. The new building is in the main street; and it is designed to be light and airy. It is a transformation from what people might expect of a homelessness centre.

For one thing, they did away with the reception desk. The layout of the reception area looks more like a café. As you enter, staff – or others in the centre – will take the steps to walk up to you. Some of the rooms upstairs are made available to other outreach services to use, to base some staff there. When an individual is ready to talk to someone, there is no labyrinthine referral process or lengthy wait to make an initial contact.

But there is one other tiny feature of that environment that speaks volumes. One member of the new staff team decided one day to bring in to the open reception area a handful of potted plants. Everybody liked them, so they brought in some more. Soon the place was as green as a garden centre; and what they found was that some of the street homeless people coming there began to help out with the watering.

It took on. Now, when one of their centre users does get a flat to move on to, they get to take with them one of these plants. The plant sits there as a reminder of the help they have had, the care they have shown and been shown. Back at the centre, these plants all around are now tokens of optimism for a new future.

Open spaces

Which takes us to another of the innovations of PIEs 2: the appreciation and conscious use of local networks and surroundings, as part of the service.

One hostel-based psychologist talks of going for a walk in the local park with one of the residents, and man with chronic schizophrenia who can be quite withdrawn and hard to reach, at the hostel. But in the park, she was amazed to find how well he knew all the animals, especially the ducks; and how he would chat freely with the parks staff. Give him a new environment to be in, and a whole new side to this man came out.

Another worker, in an outreach team, describes taking one of her 'caseload' to an appointment, in her car. What she found – and more to the point, what she noticed – was that the relationship changed. They spoke more freely as they travelled together. Where usually making eye contact is very valuable for creating a sense of relations, of value in the person, there are times when not sitting face to face can open up new territory; and it's far more practical and cheaper than the psych-analyst's couch, that cliché so beloved of cartoonists.

Another service for young people has youngsters who, after a period in the hostel to stabilise and form relationships of trust with the support staff there, continue to get their support from the same hostel staff team, as they move out to a flat of their own. (They see this as a clubhouse model, or a core-and-cluster.)

Once they used to have follow-up keyworker sessions in the youngsters' new homes; or in the counselling room at the hostel. Now they are just as likely to have these sessions in a coffee bar. It's true that there is not the privacy of a dedicated counselling room; confidentiality is a little porous. But as they told me, talking about life and problems in a coffee bar – this is normalcy for young people (and for many others too). This is the life they are helping prepare their youngsters for.

Another service, working with highly vulnerable sex workers in the north of England, encouraged group discussions between the clients. One day, as it was hot, they decided to take the discussion out, into the local park, and continue the conversation. For many, it was the first time they had used the park not to turn tricks, but as citizens, with as much right as anyone to be there. They were reclaiming the space; and the meaning of the space for them – a small step but valuable step towards healing the internalised stigma in their lives.

Incidentally, not all constructive discussion groups need to be formally a therapeutic group. In a women's drop in in Bristol, also there to provide respite and a safe space off the streets for sex workers, the staff attempted at times having talking therapy groups. No-one came. When instead they established a regular session of knitting, it was immediately popular; and there the woman talked freely about their lives, what stressed them, and how they coped.

Shared spaces

All together, these examples are a reminder that many valuable activities that are very positive for mental health, particularly in involvement in group and community activities, are not seen as 'treatment'. Sadly, the health benefits of participation in these were often only fully appreciated when described a therapy - animal assisted therapy, eco-therapy.

But this last is also a reminder that although we speak here of personal space, not all uses of space are simply individual. We now know that isolation is as bad for health as smoking, and group and community support is especially helpful to those recovering from addictions, whether chemical or behavioural. Many accommodation placements have failed because the re-housed individual missed the community of the street, where they could be somebody.

For street drinkers on a park bench, the comfort of easy acceptance of each other amongst drinkers may be skin deep and collusive; but we ignore the importance of these social bonds at our peril This, too, is a use of what we might call the 'found environment' to meet deep psychological and personal needs – for companionship; and we can learn to recognise and respect that.

Sector engagement

More commonly, though, we find services working to encourage and facilitate engagement of their service users with other valuable support services and organisations, outside their own service. In the PIEs 2 framework, we call this 'sector engagement', because to give it a name, and a place in the framework, is to give this recognition and encouragement as a valuable and a potentially intrinsic part of the work.

One CEO of a small voluntary organisation working (again) with drug-using sex workers in inner London told how much of her initial work in creating their services was with the local police force, to explain what they were doing, to give them the space and time to work with these woman, and to get them to see their charity not as a nuisance but as a valuable resource to them.

Many social housing agencies in the UK will be active in attending events to discuss local needs, gaps and barriers, and exploring how to work through them with other agencies involved. Many are highly pro-active in running events and training, not just for their own staff and service users, but for all agencies in their locality.

So we can see how the PIE approach, as it has evolved over 10+ years, is now far wider than just the attention to these immediate environments (the 'Umwelt' of each individual).

Using the rest of the framework

Even so, working with and helping to create these 'spaces of opportunity', as we call them, is still just one of the five themes or clusters of practice elements in the full PIEs framework. We call them the 'Big Five', taking that phrase from psychology, where there are said to be five key dimensions of personality that psychologists study.

The other four themes in the PIEs 2 framework are: working with and enhancing the 'psychological awareness' embedded throughout the service; emphasising 'staff training and support'; developing an attitude of 'learning and enquiry'; and finally what we call 'the Three Rs' - giving thought to the day-to-day running, the rules and the available roles for staff and for users that a service can offer, plus the overall responsiveness of the service, to make up the threesome.

This is not the time or place to go into all the possibilities here; we have, after all, an entire dedicated website through which to explore the full range of the approach. But here, we can tease out just a couple of issues, as further examples. Let's look a little closer at a couple of these PIEs 2 practice elements, that relate to Jay Levy's own working practice, in the REACH team that he manages in Western Massachusetts. These will then illustrate the ways the PIEs framework now connects with the Jay's work as he has described it in several of his earlier books, and in many videos and radio interviews.

As we've said, the PIEs approaches places great emphasise on training and support for the staff, in recognition of a growing understanding of how emotionally demanding this work can be. In one of his earlier books, this is the aspect of the PIEs framework that Jay focussed on, to stress the importance he places on supervision for his workers. Like Jay's work, the PIE approach also encourages reflective practice, both as a form of staff support – listening to their own thoughts on what they might learn – and so enhancing the responsiveness of the service. In fact, this is seen as one of the key pillars – sometimes described as the 'golden road' to developing as a PIE.

Relationships: continuity and witness

But let's also mention another element not just on the thinking but on the practice in Jay Levy's own team's work in the REACH service that does particularly well reflect and exemplify one of the Three Rs in the PIE framework: the value in thinking through the range of roles on offer in a service.

Jay has written extensively about this in his earlier books: As he describes it, the same workers that have first made contact with a homeless individual – the outreach part of their work – will continue to work with that individual as they take the first steps towards temporary - or 'interim' - housing; and the same worker will continue to work and keep in contact, as they move on, to settled accommodation.

Rather than passing the individual over to a new set of workers, and having to start over to establish the same level of trust afresh, the continuity in these working relationships that the REACH service can provide is not just a practical arrangement. It shows a marked respect for the value of the relationship.

In one of the interviews I had with Jay, we discussed how the worker is then a witness to the progress the individual has made. As with Boland's study of photo-reportage, this is affirmation as a form of support. It is comparable, clearly, to the clubhouse approach of the youth service I'd mentioned earlier. In both cases - and there are many more such examples - this on-going relationship then offers a new dimension of stability, beyond the terms of the tenancy alone.

It is a sad fact that the way so many services are funded, with tightly focussed, outcome-specified and time-limited targets to reach, actually militates against realising the value of the relationships of trust, as pivotal to success. But we'll come back to that, in a page or two.

Where to now?

The picture I have been painting here so far is one of a new spirit in homelessness services, that we in the UK and Jay and his team in the US have been exploring, each trying to identify the key features. It is one that has evolution and innovation at its heart. So these efforts are on-going, and perhaps always will be. Jay's work evolves, just as ours does here in the UK - as his new book will show.

What next, then? Let us end this essay with trying to look ahead a little; because the PIE idea, it seems, is spreading, and in three main ways.

Extending within and throughout the service

Firstly, one of the major developments in some of the more recent PIE discussions – in the informal, on-line 'forums', to which all PIElink community members are invited - has been the need for 'embedding' of the PIE approach throughout the whole of the agency, 'from top to toe', and even beyond, into work with others partners and services in the locality.

As our understanding has grown of the importance of the environment as a context, and of tackling issues in the context, so the concept of 'working with the built environment and its social spaces' has grown, from just looking at the buildings we use, to considering the surroundings and networks, to the systems and pathways, opportunities and barriers.

We have already mentioned the work that many agencies are doing in reaching out to other services in their locality, to understand better the needs and the barriers in their area. In the PIEs 2 framework, we call this 'sector engagement'. This kind of reaching out to understand includes also discussions with local commissioners and other funders, whose expectations of what services should do will form the context in which they and we must work – the business environments, so to speak.

Extending outwards, to other countries

Secondly, this idea may have begun with our observations of a radical shift in practice around the turn of this century, seen most clearly in homelessness and housing support services and at first – largely for historical reasons – mainly in the UK. But the idea is being taken up by services and governments not just across the UK, but now also in Europe. Australia is closely following.

The US and Canada may well be next. Certainly there is a significant recent re-frame in US federal government policy and funding, that now sees a useful and legitimate role for 'interim housing' and for various forms of 'recovery housing'. In the US, we see a recent re-frame of homelessness to a public health perspective - and in the words of the new HUD executive director, Jeffry Olivet, 'the causes of homelessness are systemic, not individual'.

In Canada, even some years earlier, we heard talk of 'systemic HF', that is, to see permanent housing with voluntaristic support as the long term aspiration for individuals, but with many other forms of constructive intervention possible, besides 'pure' HF practice, on the road to get there from here.

This shift means that these countries too are now looking for a broader framework of ideas and practice to bring a bigger vision to this work. A far broader account of the causes and solutions to homelessness needs a new language to get to the essence of the issues, and to the common ground of concern to do better, to work better together. It is too soon to say whether the PIE approach may be able to cross the Atlantic, and play a useful part in this development. But it's a dialogue worth continuing to open.

Extending beyond, to other fields of 'complex needs'

Firstly, these ideas, that were bubbling up and coming together at first in the new-found enthusiasm and sophistication of homelessness services, are now being found useful and being applied in a wider range of services for those with complex psychological and emotional needs.

Even in 2018, when it was being formulated, the revised PIEs framework, PIEs 2, saw this coming; and we took care to describe the essential concepts - the 'Big Five' and the fifteen more specific practice elements – in a way that did not solely refer to homelessness. Just as the precepts of pre-treatment and trauma informed care can be applied far widely, the PIE approach is potentially broad.

This means that other services facing other needs are free to explore what this spirit and this framework may have to offer them, in addressing the complexity of needs in their own sphere. It is this breadth that then allows us to talk to each other, to develop the same awareness, across platforms. This is necessary when our work requires us to find a shared vision of progress, one that bridges our areas of work, rather than the silo'ed thinking that has been part of the problem in the past.

Extending upwards, to the policy makers

As our understanding of 'the environment' widens, we come to the idea that the systems we work within are themselves social constructions. In their own way, they are also 'built environments', and they create the 'social spaces' that services must work within.

This last new direction for this dynamic new thinking may then prove to be more radical still; it is the need to communicate this enthusiasm and this commitment, and the lessons learned in services, up the chains of command, to policy makers and funders, even at national level.

Lately we have been hearing for more and more directions the claim that we do now know, pretty much, how to improve services, even within the severe resource constraints that we must live with. We have a growing sense of how to make these environments of all kinds more constructive. But now it seems to be the wider system in which all out work must operate that we must tackle.

This then brings with it a potential step change in thinking about what the full scope in the PIE approach might yet be. On the PIElink itself (see below), there are pages asking whether, at some point, we might even want a new version of the PIE language, that takes these same ideas on what works, on what we are learning and what we now need, up another level.

This might mean another version of the PIEs framework that re-casts these ideas for a more extensive policy shift – in effect, a 'PIEs 3'. Or it may be that the PIE approach and the PIE spirit that underlies it may need something else entirely, a still wider coalition of the positive voices and the messages we hear, when governments listen to service providers and service users.

Further pathways

Both Pretreatment and PIE, in their different spheres, have articulated the core issues and skills in engagement. Pretreatment looks mainly at the micro-social level of 1-1 interactions, and asks us to fully respect there the subjective, experiential world of the individual, to engage first and foremost with 'where they are at'. The PIEs approach by comparison looks mainly at the meso-social level, where organisations operate; and then asks us to consider every aspect of a service, to ask how far it helps us to deliver the engagements and the transitions we hope to see.

It might then seem that the PIEs approach is asking us to see the inner world of service users from the outside, but it is not. It is asking us to use our own natural capacity for empathy, to relate and connect, just as pretreatment asks us to consider the ecology of issues for the individual, to respect their own investment in the environment of their lived experience – their 'Umwelt'. This is co-production on a 1-1 scale.

Nor does Pretreatment ignore the environment. A passage in *'Cross-cultural Dialogues'* sums this up well :

'....Similar to PIE, the term "environment" is defined broadly and encompasses not only the physical environment, but also interpersonal aspects, exposure to ideas, values and rules that govern social structure, other participants, and even the different phases of a client-worker relationship.' (p228)

At times of change, when we may be assisting someone in what we hope will be a successful transition and adaptation to new relationships, ideas, services, resources, treatment and housing, we must be most aware of what Jay calls 'ecological considerations'.

But what this alerts us to is that these considerations were in fact already there, for each individual, before we attempt to make contacts and offer new possibilities and opportunities. As Jay puts it in an earlier book: '*It is remarkable to think that my offer of help can easily be seen as disruptive or unsettling to their survival routines.*' (p. 49, italics in the original, in *Pretreatment Guide to Homeless Outreach and Housing First*)

Pretreatment calls for a heightened sensitivity to the hidden costs for the individual of the changes we ask them to make. Simply ignoring these to focus solely on the 'outcomes' that the service is contracted to deliver may be the major reason for failure of a contact, a treatment programme, or a tenancy.

But now we need to explore how far we can go in using the PIEs approach and framework in looking upwards, at whole systems; and we look further still, at the macro-social world of policies and policy makers, politicians and opinion formers, influencers of all kinds in professional bodies, regulators and the information services

There is also a still wider environment in which humanity struggles to find better ways to tackle the huge problems that, it seems, are largely of our own making. Where and how we can ever hope to translate these values, insights and energies into a still more ambition vision remains a moot point.

But we live in hope.

CHAPTER 10

UNFINISHED BUSINESS

This collection ends with a non-ending. To stay true to the 'unfinalisable' idea, this last chapter is not an essay itself, but a comment and a confirmation that the PIElink site now has a suite of pages where we can continue the discussion, and develop new material, new ideas, new directions.

At the time of writing, the route to this section of the website is the page is called 'PIE publications'. There you will find a link firstly to a page specifically on this book; and from there, there are further pages for each chapter, with more examples, links to related pages, library items, video etc.

You will also find a page (and many subsidiary pages) for another new book which is being published alongside this one. '*Psychologically informed environments from the ground up: service design for complex needs*' is more like a primer, an introduction to the whole approach, the history, the PIEs framework (both PIEs One and PIEs 2.0), the Pizazz etc.

You will also find here a page and some links for '*Cross-cultural dialogues on homelessness; from pre-treatment strategies to psychologically informed environments*', the book co-edited with Jay Levy some years back. Through the book/website linkage used here, this earlier book now too connects with a lot of very new material on 'American PIE', with Jay's new books, and the forum discussions.

Going back even further, there are some excerpts from '*Complex trauma and its effects: perspectives on creating an environment for recovery*', a much earlier collection, co-edited with Rex Haigh. The first section of that book covers the nature of trauma and compound trauma from a wide range of perspectives, echoing several of the chapters here; and the essays in the central section cover a wide range of services and sectors, reflecting the much wider scope that the PIEs 2.0 framework now reaches.

If this book/website linkage takes off as an idea, there will hopefully be other books that we can publicise via 'PIE publications'. But even if not, the material on the site itself can continue to 'un-finalise' the writings here...

And finally, for now...

Finally there needs to be a comment here on work that is so unfinished it has barely begun. There are a number of suggestions for new areas for the PIEs approach - and for the website - to grow into. One that I have mentioned in the chapter of pretreatment is potential to be explored in the notion of the Umwelt, and the light that this may shed on neuroscience and developmental psychology.

Another that stands out is the potential in the PIEs approach to address broader systems, and to play a role in current calls for more systemic change. This is actually the point at which the *'Psychologically informed environments from the ground up'* book ends.

But equally significant in the long run may be the efforts to now develop research using the PIEs framework, and the challenge to narrow, out-dated and inappropriate methodologies that have held back exploration of the impact of environments of all kinds on human experience.

So this last chapter here is not really a full essay at all, but is best seen as a portal to another world - in this case, to the PIElink website, and to the world beyond, where these explorations and discussions can continue, and be fully unfinalisable.

AFTERTHOUGHTS

Sometimes the light's all shining on me.
Other times I can barely see.
Lately it occurs to me.
What a long strange trip it's been.....
      The Grateful Dead

Time rolls on; and a fairly constant stream of new ideas, new opportunities unfolds. In the months before finalising this selection of essays to publish - there are so many I just do not have time to complete - I had come across the concept of the 'Umwelt'. I suspect this will be seriously valuable in future, in linking our human experience with the biological world, in a new key.

I came across this notion just in time to weave it into the story and analysis that I was then writing of the common ground between PIEs and pre-treatment; but not in time to include it in the (by then near-complete) essay on the bio-psycho-social environment, where it very clearly should go. That writing must now wait for another time.

Then, in the very last few days before I was ready to send this text to the printers, a colleague sent me an article on 'autoethnography' from the August issue of The Psychologist.

Since here I have not been afraid to refer to my own life and intellectual journeying, I wonder now if this book, so full of my own meandering interests, is itself an example of this kind of writing. Perhaps not; but there are a couple of quotes from this article that I should like to share...

* * *

What is autoethnography?

'Autoethnography is an 'autobiographical genre of writing and research that displays multiple layers of consciousness, connecting the personal to the cultural'...

Autoethnographers undertake research that seeks to affectively and intellectually explore something in an expansive manner that renders the self in context.

As such, autoethnography is profoundly psycho-social and cherishes a single person's perspective(s) as capable of adding to academic scholarship. It refuses to distil that knowledge into a write-up that conforms to the rules of academic psychology, 'keep[ing] the complexities of human experience intact, [in order] to place the ache back in scholars' abstractions'.

Mainstream psychology, interested as it is in channelling uniqueness into sameness, enjoys enormous visibility by virtue of its claims to nomothetic knowledge about human behaviour.....

Anyhow, autoethnography capitalises on those thoughts, unlike the research traditions that shoehorn, bracket, or fail to even notice them.

I am done spending precious class time teaching brands of qualitative analysis at the expense of truly cultivating foundational research skills such as playfulness, noncertainty, affective fluency, trusting intuition, and refusing to treat the published literature as more worthy of attention than the knowledge that lives in art and rituals, our relationships, and our bodies.

Let there be chaos.'

Miltos Hadjiosif,
9th August 2023

* * *

Amen to that.
The grin remains.

ABOUT THE AUTHOR

Robin Johnson is a former therapeutic community social therapist, mental health social worker, author, researcher, data and policy analyst, editor, and now 'content provider'.

While working as UK national lead on mental health and housing for the National Social Inclusion Programme, his role included liaising closely with the Department of Health and the Department of Communities; and with the Royal College of Psychiatrists on the 'Enabling Environments' programme.

During this time Robin suggested the term 'psychologically informed environments' to describe the creative practice then emerging in homelessness services in the UK. In the years since then, he and his colleagues have refined these initial observations into a dynamic working framework for the design, development and self-assessment of effective support services for people with complex needs of all kinds.

He created the PIElink as a resource for PIEs, was the first editor/curator and wrote much of the pages material, and managed the forums up until 2023, when he began handing over to the new team.

Now trying hard to (semi-) retire, he lives in Cornwall, where he spends his time writing, gardening and singing, and plays a baritone saxophone with more enthusiasm than skill.

www.ingramcontent.com/pod-product-compliance
Lightning Source LLC
Chambersburg PA
CBHW071711020426
42333CB00017B/2218